FROM THE QUR'AN TO CONVERSION A SPIRITUAL JOURNEY

A Study on the Learning Process of the Qur'an and Arabic Language Among Female Muslim Converts From Mexico and Colombia

GABRIELA MONDRAGON

INDIA · SINGAPORE · MALAYSIA

ISBN
Paperback 979-8-89588-668-7
Hardcase 979-8-89632-845-2

Dedication

For all the Muslim converts around the world who choose to study the Holy Qur'an in its original language. May Allah reward your effort and dedication. Ameen.

All thanks and praises are for our Creator, Allah subhana wa ta'ala who has given us the guidance of Islam and instills in us the motivation and perseverance to access His holy book, the Qur'an.

I extend my deep gratitude to my mother, Gabriela Meza, who instilled in me a passion for life and the courage to constantly venture into learning new things, facing fear head-on with bravery and determination. My love and my gratitude for my husband, Mohamed Okasha, without his support I could not do this work.

I also thank my reviewers for dedicating their time and effort to read and correct my manuscript, Dr. Arely Medina and Ustadh Omar Weston.

And my sincere gratitude goes to the eight women who chose to answer my questions and share with me their valuable experiences in learning the Arabic language and everything necessary to access the Holy Qur'an in its original language.

Sincerely,

Gabriela Mondragón.

Abstract

Why do some Muslim converts set the goal of approaching the Qur'an in Arabic, its original language? This research is about the learning process of the Arabic language and the recitation of the Qur'an among female Muslim converts from Mexico and Colombia. The objective is to explore their learning experiences, including their study opportunities, challenges, obstacles, and frustrations, as well as the positive effects and significant achievements. The research is qualitative with an action research design. Eight interviews were conducted with convert women, five from Mexico and three from Colombia. The theoretical framework aims to be holistic, incorporating an andragogical model (Knowles, 2001), intrinsic motivation (Cook & Artino, 2016), voluntary and fluid attention (Bruya & Tang, 2018; 2021), and emotional regulation (Wadlinger & Isaacowitz, 2011). The intention is to contribute to the understanding of the Arabic learning process and Qur'an recitation techniques among female Muslim converts, and to offer suggestions that help overcome challenges and difficulties. It concludes that Muslim converts construct and strengthen their religious identity through learning and memorization, possess intrinsic motivation, and demonstrate how they deploy attention and concentration through repetitions and/or recitation of the Qur'an, which helps regulate emotions. Their understanding of the Qur'an is facilitated through Spanish or English, as they do not necessarily learn Arabic for communicative purposes. Technology and digitalization facilitate learning and help them achieve their study goals. The isolation during COVID-19 had a positive impact on their learning.

Keywords: Qur'an, Arabic, *Tajweed*, recitation, learning, conversion to Islam, Islam in Latin America.

Preface

In the name of Allah, the Most Merciful, the Most Compassionate. Praise be to Allah, Lord and Creator of all worlds. I bear witness that there is no deity worthy of worship except Allah, and I bear witness that Muhammad is His servant and messenger. I accept that Islam is the final religion established by Allah on earth and that the Qur'an is the last of His revealed sacred books. I believe in the unseen world, in Allah, in the angels, and in the *jinn*. I believe in the Day of Judgment, in divine predestination, and that Allah sent prophets and messengers to humanity to establish monotheism. I believe in all the books revealed by Allah.

Regarding some abbreviations and their meanings: When writing texts that reference the Prophet (saw) and Allah (swt), the code of ethics and Islamic tradition is to offer salutations each time their names are mentioned. For example, when mentioning the name of Allah, one says, "Praise be to Him," and when mentioning the Prophet Muhammad, one states, "May peace and blessings of Allah be upon him." Considering that this may interrupt the flow of reading, salutations will be abbreviated in parentheses as explained below.

When referring to Allah (Praise be to Him), it will be accompanied by '(swt)', which in transliteration reads 'subhana wa ta'ala' and means 'The Most High' or 'The Elevated'. It can also be understood as the one who is above creation or who does not belong to it, but rather creation belongs to Him (swt). When mentioning or referring to the Prophet Muhammad (peace and blessings be upon him), it will be accompanied by '(saw)', which in transliteration reads 'sala Allahu aleihi wa salam' and means 'may the peace and blessings of Allah be upon him'. In the case of the angel Gabriel (peace be upon him), it will be accompanied by '(as)', which in transliteration reads 'aleihi salam' and means 'may peace be upon him'. When speaking of any companion of the Prophet (saw), the name will be mentioned followed by salutations; for example, 'Omar Bin Al-Khattab (raa)', which in transliteration reads 'radi Allahu anhu' and means 'may Allah be pleased with him or her'.

I would also like to thank the reader for approaching the reading of this humble work, which aims to investigate the process of learning to read and recite the Qur'an, specifically the learning of the Arabic language and the rules of recitation called *Tajweed*. This study is conducted within the complex context of conversion to Islam. For Muslim converts, learning to read and recite the Qur'an is part of the religious rituals of worship and praise to The Most High (swt) and part of building our Muslim identity.

Contents

List of Figures

List of Tables

Introduction

Muslims in Mexico and Colombia make up less than 1% of the total population in both countries (PEW Research Center, 2012). Part of this group consists of immigrants from various Muslim countries, while another percentage comprises Mexican and Colombian converts to Islam. These converts are adults with the capacity to make decisions about their lives, possessing valuable prior knowledge and diverse experiences that cannot be ignored when studying their journey of conversion and learning to practice the Islamic religion. This study focuses on the learning of the Arabic language and the recitation of the Qur'an among female Muslim converts from Mexico and Colombia. The purpose is to gather different experiences related to learning Arabic to read and understand the Qur'an and to study the rules of recitation established in *Tajweed*. The objectives are (1) to collect learning experiences, (2) to identify challenges and difficulties, (3) to identify positive effects, and (4) to gather suggestions with the aim of contributing to the creation and development of educational and didactic projects appropriate for Latino communities.

Why is it important to read the Qur'an in Arabic and learn to recite it? Why do some Muslim converts set the goal of approaching the Sacred Book in its original language? Throughout the Sacred Book, there are 10 verses about the revelation of the Qur'an being in the Arabic language; one example is in *Surah Ar-Ra'd* (The Thunder)

13:37: "Thus, then, we bestowed from on high this (divine writ) as an ordinance in the Arabic tongue" (translation by Muhammad Asad, 1980). Another verse invites believers to recite it slowly and melodiously, as seen in *Surah Al Muzzamil* (The Wrapped One) 73:4: "(...) and recite the Qur'an calmly and distinctly, with thy mind attuned to its meaning" (translation by Muhammad Asad, 1980). The Islamic tradition of learning to read Arabic and reciting the Qur'an melodiously originated from these verses.

Thus, The Qur'an becomes the center of this present study. It is a book in classical Arabic, consisting of 114 chapters known as *suras*; the correct term in plural for several suras is *suwar*, but we have Latinized the word as 'suras'. Some names of the Qur'an include: 'The Book' *Al Kitab*, 'The Guidance' *Al Huda*, 'The Light' *Al Nur*, 'The Recitation' *Al Qur'an*, 'Mercy' *Ar Rahma*, 'The Criterion' *Al Furqan*, 'The Cure' *Al Shifá*, 'Reminder' *Al Dhikr*, 'Confirmed Writing' *Musaddiq*, 'The Word of Allah' *Kalamullah*, 'Revelation' *Tanzil*, 'Inspiration' *Wahy*, 'The Truth' *Al Haqq*, 'The Good News' *Al Bushra*, 'The Warning' *An Nadhir*, 'A Sufficient Message' *Balagh*. These names can be found within the text of the Qur'an itself.

The tradition of learning and reciting the Sacred Book in Arabic extends to the various geographical areas where new Muslims are located. The convert to Islam begins to be part of the community of *'Iqra'*, meaning someone who is constantly reading and learning, both from the Qur'an and from other books, as well as from reading and interpreting their environment and reality. What is the perspective of female Muslim converts regarding the Islamic tradition of learning to read Arabic and recite the Qur'an melodiously? How is the experience of female Muslim converts, particularly in Mexico and Colombia, as they approach the Qur'an in Arabic to read, understand, and recite it? What challenges and difficulties do they face in this task? How and where do they find opportunities to study Arabic and recite the Qur'an? What are the positive effects of doing so? What suggestions or actions do these Muslim women propose to overcome the challenges and difficulties in the process of learning Arabic and recitation? These are the questions that this study aims to answer.

The concern for this topic arose with my own conversion to Islam in Mexico City in October 2013 while reading the translation of the Qur'an (Melara Navío, 1996). The copy had two columns: the left side is the Spanish translation, and the right is in Arabic. I found myself looking at the Arabic letters with a desire to recognize them, read them, and understand the meaning of each word. A year later, I traveled to Cairo, Egypt, where I learned the basics of the Arabic language and the rules of recitation, or *Tajweed*. Throughout my journey, I have attended in-person classes in Egypt and Malaysia, taken online classes from Mexico, and engaged in self-study in various places where I have lived. Daily interactions with my Egyptian in-laws have gradually allowed me to develop communication skills. The reason I am conducting this research is to explore the experiences of learning among other convert Muslim woman with a similar background.

This present work is divided into several sections. First, general concepts are presented for better understanding, such as *I'qra'*, Arabic, *Tajweed*, and *Tarteel*, as well as Qur'anic concepts of the mind, the heart, and the anatomy of the voice as elements involved in the learning of Qur'anic recitation. The theoretical-methodological framework reviews andragogy, motivation, and emotion regulation as the theoretical basis for interpreting the results. Finally, the findings of the research are presented, followed by conclusions.

Chapter 1

General Concepts

1.1. *I'qra'*: Between Reading and Reciting

I'qra' is an Arabic word written as a command. Its etymological root is q-r-a' (qara'a), which literally means "to read." It was the first word that the prophet of the Muslims, Muhammad (saw), received in revelation in the cave of Hira, Mecca. I will attempt to define it, according to commentators and translators of the Qur'an consulted mainly from the *IslamCity.org*[1] database. *I'qra'* has other meanings, through which I will try to clarify and classify how we can access[2] the Qur'an.

1 IslamiCity.org is a nonprofit organization founded in 1995, operated by HADI (Human Assistance and Development International) with the registration number (EIN: 95-4348674). Its Qur'an webpage was used, which contains an extensive compilation of different English translations, as well as commentaries. This resource facilitated the consultation and comparison of various translations.

2 I use the verb 'access' to refer to the different ways in which a convert approaches the sacred Qur'an, and I will subsequently explain what 'accessing the Qur'an' means within the context of Muslim converts.

The word *I'qra'* is translated into English as 'to read,' 'to recite,' and 'to proclaim'. Yusuf Ali comments that the word can have several meanings: to read, to recite, to repeat, or to proclaim. In Spanish, Julio Cortés translates it as 'recite' (Cortés, 2005), while Abdel Ghani Melara Navío and Isa García translate it as 'read' (García, 2013; Melara Navío, 1996). *I'qra'* was a command directed to the Prophet (saw) but also to all Muslims around the world, regardless of their origin, time, or mother tongue (Hosein, 2020). Reading, reciting, reflecting on, and understanding the meanings of the sacred Qur'an becomes a task or duty for every Muslim.

Most people, non-Arab speakers, access the translation of the Qur'an as an experiment (Al-Qwidi, 2002), but what is the process of accessing the Qur'an in its original language, which is Arabic? Is it a decisive and directed decision and action? Or is it something experimental? Translations of the Qur'an into Spanish are the primary source of access to the Book for Spanish-speaking converts, but sooner or later, every Muslim needs to access the Qur'an in its original language, at least to learn the necessary *surah* to fulfill the obligatory prayers that must be performed five times a day[3].

Reciting the Qur'an requires constant practice and perseverance. However, the word 'practice' is too ambiguous and too wide to describe what a convert needs to undertake to access the Qur'an in its original language. In the context of Latino Muslim converts, I would define the 'practice' of Qur'an recitation as constant repetitions of a letter, a word, a phrase, an *ayah* (verse), or an entire *surah* of the Qur'an as many times as necessary until achieving correct pronunciation and applying the rules of recitation and if possible, memorization.

3 One of the religious obligations of the Muslims all over the world is to pray five times per day, according to the teachings of the prophet Mohammad (saw), which includes at least *surah Al Fatiha*, The Opening Chapter of the Qur'an.

Ideally, while the student repeats, someone else listens and corrects the apprentice. Through constant repetitions, fluency and retention in memory are achieved, although not necessarily understanding. Understanding comes through the study of the Arabic language.

1.2. Arabic: The Language of the Qur'an

« وَكَذَٰلِكَ أَنزَلْنَاهُ حُكْماً عَرَبِيًّا » (سورة الرَّعْد ٣٧)

The language of the Qur'an is Arabic, as evidenced in *Surah Ar-Ra'd* (The Thunder 13:37): "Thus have We revealed the Qur'an in Arabic[4]." The arrival of the Qur'an made the Arabic language always relevant and alive (Alkhateeb, 2014). Arabic is one of the Semitic languages, along with Aramaic and Hebrew (Aboelezz, 2015; Bishop, 1998; Macdonald, 2008). It is likely that the Arabic language itself is a form of artistic expression, and Arabic poetry became *de facto* art of pre-Islamic Arabs (Alkhateeb, 2014).

However, written language was not the norm in Arab society; oral tradition prevailed, making memorization sufficient to transmit stories, genealogy, values, and wisdom from one generation to the next. Pre-Islamic Arabs were capable of memorizing poems of hundreds of lines. This memorization ability proved to be of great importance when the Qur'an was revealed (Alkhateeb, 2014). In the Islamic context, 'memorization' refers to the process of storing in one's memory, either partially or completely, the Sacred Book in its original language, which we call Qur'anic memorization. Generally, new Muslims begin by memorizing the *surah* that opens the book, *Al-Fatiha*, which consists of seven *ayaat* (verses), and it is obligatory to

4 Similar evidences are at Corán: 12:2, 13:37, 16:103, 20:113, 26:195,39:28,41:3, 42:7, 43:3, 46:12.

recite it in every prayer; this is the minimum that a practicing Muslim must memorize.

Currently, the Arabic language is classified into three categories: Classical Arabic, derived from the Qur'an and pre-Islamic poetry; Standard Arabic, used in formal and diplomatic contexts where new terms are included; and the Arabic dialects that developed and evolved through interactions with other languages and cultures, a phenomenon known as diglossia (Aboelezz, 2015; Bishop, 1998). Learning the Arabic language and understanding the meaning of each word is a cognitive and educational activity—a type of knowledge that is not strictly necessary for reciting the Qur'an but is vital for understanding it. Learning the rules of Qur'anic recitation is called *Tajweed*, while reciting it melodiously and with intonation is referred to as *Tarteel*. The learning of the language goes hand in hand with recitation to achieve the ability to read, recite, and comprehend the Qur'an.

The letters and sounds of the Arabic language have also been transcribed using the alphabet, which is called transliteration. Transliteration is a graphemic transcription, which consists of representing each grapheme of the 'source text' with another in the graphemic system of the 'target text', so that it can be reversible, ensuring that the sound represented in the 'target text', in this case, Spanish, comes as close as possible to the sound of the 'source text', which is Arabic (Corriente, 2002).

1.3. *Tajweed*: Giving Each Qur'anic Letter Its Right

Tajweed is one part of Qur'anic studies that explains the rules and norms of recitation for reading the Qur'an correctly (Umm Najm, 2013). Literally, *Tajweed* means 'to do well' in Islamic terminology.

It refers to giving each letter of the Qur'an its right place of articulation in the mouth, its time and characteristics, observing the rules of recitation such as elongations, stops, and silences. Reciting the Qur'an (without understanding it) involves different types of knowledge. First, knowledge of the alphabet, each letter, its forms, and its movements. Second, the rules to follow and knowing how to apply and pronounce them. Third, we need to know our body and how it works, which primarily involves physiological activities.

Each letter has its own characteristics, and giving them their right means considering their pronunciation features and not omitting any sound, and this is clear in the workbooks of *Tajweed* (Umm Máyid, 2015). Start studying *Tajweed,* having the basic knowledge of the Arabic language is a must, meaning they should know the Arabic alphabet, as well as the vowels and other symbols such as pauses, elongations, etc. (Colón, 2014; Czerepinski, 2000).

The traditional or conventional method of teaching and learning *Tajweed* is in a classroom setting with a teacher who indicates the correct way to pronounce each letter of a word or phrase from the Qur'an along with its characteristics (Alagrami & Eljazzar, 2020; Muhammad et al., 2012; Osborne, 2020; Wahid et al., 2019)—whether it has a vowel, elongation, silence, or a doubled letter, among other aspects. Currently, technological resources, online classes, distance learning, and sometimes asynchronous methods are being used to learn techniques for reading and reciting the Qur'an (Alagrami & Eljazzar, 2020; Muhammad et al., 2012; Osborne, 2020; Wahid et al., 2019).

1.4. *Tarteel* and Melody

«وَرَتِّلِ الْقُرْءَانَ تَرْتِيلاً» (سورة الْمُزَّمِّل ٤)

Reciting the Qur'an with *Tarteel* is the art of reciting the Qur'an slowly and melodiously, in a rhythmic manner. In *Surah Al Muzzammil* (The Wrapped One 73:4), it says: "and recite the Qur'an slowly and melodiously." Considering that at the moment of the revelation, Arab poetry was at its peak of eloquence and beauty, the Qur'an arrived in the form of poetic recitation as well, surpassing the poetry that the pre-Islamic Arabs had created up to that point (Alkhateeb, 2014), which was considered a miracle by itself since the Prophet Mohammad (saw) didn't know how to write or read.

The instrument used for reciting the Qur'an is the voice. To achieve a melodious recitation, one must know how to use this instrument to produce the desired sounds. Training the voice and the muscles of the mouth is a physical endeavor; it requires constant practice, developing vocal and breathing techniques. The art of Qur'anic recitation is technically executed with the vocal instrument, but the mind, heart, and entire body are involved in its correct execution.

1.4.1. The Mind in the Qur'an

How is the mind involved in the recitation of the sacred Qur'an with *Tajweed* and *Tarteel*, as well as in the learning of Arabic? It is important to differentiate between the mind and the physical brain. The mind is defined as something intangible that resides in the physical brain, which is a mass located in the head. The mind is correlated with brain and cognitive processes and is where thinking, reasoning, learning, attention, concentration, consciousness, memory, imagination, and dreams occur. Different mental processes are classified into conscious, unconscious, and procedural (Smart, 2022). Generally, the mind receives data from external sources (its environment and other people) and internal sources (the body or products of mental processes).

The deconstruction of religious identity prior to conversion to Islam occurs in the mind with these mental processes (Mondragón, 2023). The decision to convert, learning, the construction of identity, interpretation of lived experiences, memory, all of this information is processed in the mind. The perspective of traditional psychology is that all these processes happen exclusively in the brain, but according to Qur'anic evidence, there are processes also performed by the heart, such as the creation of intentions, decision-making, discernment, and understanding. Definitions and evidence are presented in the following section regarding the heart.

In the Qur'an, the mind is related to intelligence, reasoning, and understanding. The word *aql* appears 49 times in the sacred text (for example, Qur'an 67:10, 10:16, 11:51, 12:109) and is translated as intellect, reasoning, or thought, where cognitive, learning, and psychological processes occur and are related to brain activities. In the Qur'an, it is considered that *aql*, or intellect, has a strong relationship with the heart, *qalb*, due to the cognitive capabilities and functions of discernment and decision-making that, according to the Qur'an, can also be performed with the heart (Şeker, 2012). Other Qur'anic words used for mind, intelligence, or reasoning include *jilm* (e.g., Qur'an 52:32), translated as 'mind,' *jiyr* (e.g., Qur'an 89:5), translated as 'understanding', and *nuja* (e.g., Qur'an 20:54, 20:128), translated as 'intelligence', all three considered synonyms of *aql* within the Qur'an (Şeker, 2012).

1.4.2. The Heart in the Qur'an

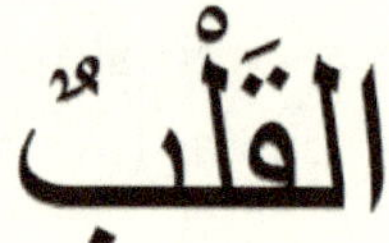

The heart is the central organ of the circulatory system located on the left side of the chest within the thoracic cavity, and it is responsible for pumping and circulating blood throughout the body. The heart is an organ that can be trained and conditioned to become stronger, much like what high-performance athletes do or anyone looking to maintain stable health. Similarly, the heart can be trained to strengthen faith (Haque, 2017; Şeker, 2012).

The word 'heart' appears 137 times in the Qur'an. The Arabic word for this vital organ is *qalb*. The Arabic etymological root is q-l-b (qalaba), which means 'to transform, change, alter, transmute'. Thus, it is inferred that the heart *qalb* is something that can transform and change rapidly (Haque, 2017; Olatoye, 2013). Some verses of the Qur'an that refer to the heart include in *Surah At-Tawbah* (The Repentance 9:87): "(...) their hearts have been sealed, so they cannot grasp the truth." At *Surah al-Anfal* (The Spoils of War 8:24) refers: "(...) and know that God intervenes between man and (the desires) of his heart" (Interpretation to English by Muhammad Asad, 1980). A last example is located at *Surah Ar-Ra'd* (The Thunder 13:28): "The hearts of the believers find peace in the remembrance of Allah (swt). Is it not with the remembrance of Allah that hearts find peace?" The word *fuad* or *fa'ida* is also translated as heart and is mentioned 16 times in the Qur'an (e.g., Qur'an 6:110, 14:37, 6:113, 46:26) and denotes warmth, even extreme heat. This term can refer to the heart when it 'burns' from painful experiences, as well as because it is constantly in motion and always warm—reflecting the dynamic nature of the heart (Şeker, 2012).

The word *sadr* appears 40 times in the Qur'an, which is translated as 'chest' (e.g., Qur'an 6:125, 35:38, 11:5, 10:57, 31:23, 3:119). It is defined as the part located between a person's neck and navel, described as 'the chief' or 'the commander' of the whole body (Şeker, 2012). It is the place that receives the first impact from the context or unexpected situations, where emotions are generated, needs are felt, and it is where whispers and suspicions are received, as well as where arrogance and carnal desires reside. It is also in the chest where belief in Allah (swt) is found, where faith and spirituality develop and grow, and where religious knowledge is kept (Şeker, 2012).

Allah (swt) describes three types of hearts in the Qur'an: the healthy (e.g., Qur'an 26:89-90, 37:84), the sick (Qur'an 8:49), and the dead (Olatoye, 2013). The healthy heart is one that has a deep love for Allah (swt), cares about pleasing and worshipping Him, and is free from the ties of this world. A person with a healthy heart possesses tranquility and peace. The dead heart is the opposite; it is when it completely rejects Allah (swt) and any form of worship. It is described as a dry, hard heart infertile (Qur'an 2:74), (Olatoye, 2013). In the Qur'an, the dead heart is associated with disbelief in Allah (swt). The sick heart is one that believes in Allah (swt), seeks His pleasure but is attached to material and carnal desires, constantly fluctuating in faith in Allah (swt), and strives to avoid what has been forbidden, such as major sins like idolatry and oppression. It also endeavors to perform more acts of worship (such as praying, fasting, remembering Allah, making supplications, reading the Qur'an, doing good deeds, helping others, etc.).

According to the Qur'an, the heart can be veiled (6:25), blocked or enclosed (47:24), deviated (3:8), shaken and stirred (79:8), hardened (6:43), sealed (2:7), and can be blind (22:46). However, it can also be good (8:70), can perceive with the 'eye of the heart', meaning that the heart has the ability to perceive and 'see' (22:46), has the capacity to reason and understand (7:179). It can be guided (3:8), can have faith (58:22), can be soft or can be softened and calm (39:23), there are tranquil or relieved hearts (8:10), it can be strengthened (18:14), can be humble through the remembrance of Allah (57:16), and can find satisfaction in the remembrance of Allah (13:28) (Cook & Yucel, 2022; Şeker, 2012). The heart is also the generator of intentions and is involved in the decision-making process (Olatoye, 2013).

1.4.3. The Body and the Anatomy of the Voice

The body is fully involved in the execution of the recitation of the Qur'an. As a ritualistic practice, a Muslim needs to know about the physical purification before starting the study or recitation of the Qur'an. There are two types, one is minor purification called *ghudu* and the other is major called *ghusul*. The procedures can be found in any guide for new Muslims. Starting by pronouncing *Bismillahi Rahmani Raheem* (in the name of Allah, the Most Merciful, the Most Compassionate). The *ghudu* encompasses cleaning with clean water the hands, mouth, nose, arms, ears, head, and feet three times starting by the right side and then the left part, while the *ghusul* includes all the previous, plus a shower of the complete body starting with the right side and then the left, finishing by watering three times the head with all hair. The purification of the intention while doing all of this physical ritual is important and vital for all sincere Muslims, which is to approach the Qur'an with the intention to worship Allah (swt), to respect his Sacred Book, and to learn from its wisdom.

The posture of the body, observing the correct position of the head, neck, chest, and abdomen, contributes to the control of breathing and modulation of the voice for sound production (Ancos, 2009; Torres, 2013). One needs to feel comfortable, even with the fabrics of the cloth and the type of seat or standing while reciting the Qur'an. It is also important to understand the anatomy of the voice to produce clear, modulated, and melodic sounds and the air that one needs to inhale and exhale (Ancos, 2009; Fort, 2017; Torres, 2013).

The anatomy of the voice consists of three systems: the respiratory system, which propels the air out and includes the trachea, lungs, bronchi, and diaphragm. The phonatory system is where the sound passes and comprises the entire vocal tract, nasal passages, larynx, vocal cords, mouth, tongue, teeth, and lips. Additionally, the ear is important, as auditory training helps us fine-tune the sounds. The resonating system is formed by the cavities and openings through which sound travels and vibrates, consisting of the nasal cavity, oral cavity, soft palate, thoracic cavity, facial and cranial cavities; however, in reality, sound can travel and vibrate through the shoulders, body, and limbs (Ancos, 2009; Torres, 2013). (See diagram 1.1).

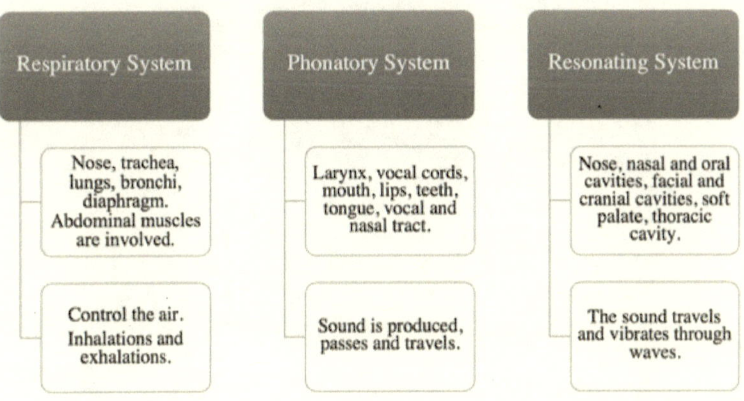

Figure 1.1. *Components of the Anatomy of the Voice.*

Learning of Qur'anic recitation implies exploring and scrutinizing everything that makes up the anatomy of the voice. The points of articulation of Arabic letters allow for the articulatory phonetics of the Qur'an. The points of articulation are defined by the manner and place of articulation of the sound of each letter, and to successfully recite The Book, it is vital to know where and how to pronounce sounds that have no equivalent in Spanish, English, or any other language (Serrano, 2013).

What we see in Figure 1.2 is basically the point of exit or articulation for each letter of the Arabic language. For example, to pronounce the letter 'mim', the lips are closed, just like the letter M in Spanish and English. If we want to pronounce the vowels A, I, U, the sound comes directly from the throat, clean and direct, similar to when the doctor asks a child to say 'A' to check the mouth or throat.

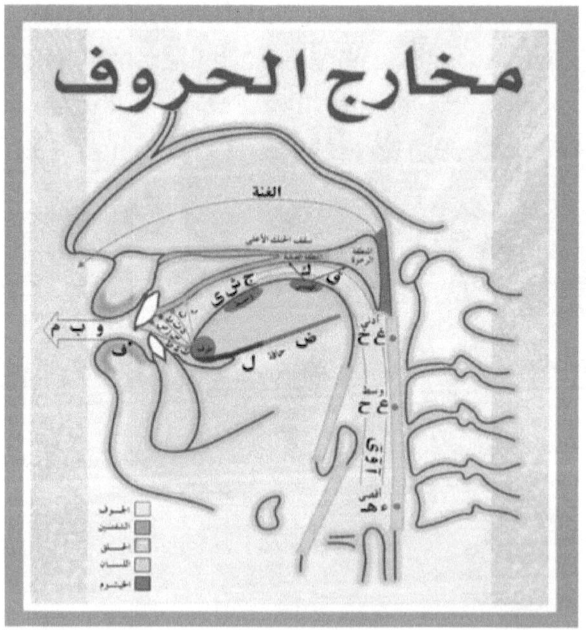

Figure 1.2. *Points of Articulation of Arabic Letters*

I'm paraphrasing the words of Professor Victoria De Ancos (2009) in the context of *Tajweed*. Understanding the body is essential for producing correct sound and positioning the voice according to each letter and its characteristics, including any movements. This involves applying pauses, silences, and elongations, activating the breath, and using the mechanisms of the mouth and articulation organs. The inhaled air should be transformed into melodic and rhythmic sound. I continue to contextualize Ancos's (2009) singing technique in our study: the flow of air is measured in the mouth, calculating the necessary amount for each phrase according to the rules of Qur'anic recitation. This release of air and sound is calculated so that over time and with practice, the reciter learns how much air is needed to complete a specific phrase or full verses. Ultimately, this also requires proper articulation through the letters and their movements and sound characteristics.

Chapter 2

Background, Theoretical Framework and Methodology

2.1. Research Supporting the Discussion

The language of the Qur'an is Arabic; however, to make it accessible to a larger number of people, various translations have been made. It has been digitalized, and electronic applications have been developed for different needs. Below, I present some academic foundations that have recorded some of the achievements. For example, there is a mobile application for the deaf using sign language in Arabic, called 'Teyban Qur'an App' (Al Isharah, 2022; Smartech Solutions, 2022). The British Muslim community is developing a Qur'an project in sign language, 'The British Sign Language Project' (Al Isharah, 2022). The Qur'an has also been translated into Braille in Arabic, English, and Ukrainian (Abualkishik & Omar, 2008), all with the aim of allowing individuals with auditory or visual impairments, or those who are neurodivergent, to access the Qur'an and be able to read it, to recite it aloud or read it through sign language.

Some research was found in Malaysia on teaching strategies for the Qur'an using sign language (Mohd Daud et al., 2012). There is another study concerning the perceptions of mothers of deaf children about Qur'anic education in Malaysia (Ghadim et al., 2013) and auditory therapy through the recitation of the Qur'an as treatment for children with autism (Mohamad et al., 2013). While accessibility to the Qur'an for individuals with disabilities is not the purpose of this study, I considered it important to mention it as part of the research conducted and the efforts of Islamic institutions to make the Qur'an accessible to as many people as possible.

Some studies regarding the reading and recitation of the Holy Qur'an include the lack of recitation among Muslims themselves (Allah S. N. et al., 2020). In this study, the authors, who are of Malay origin, outline the reasons why Islamic societies have abandoned the recitation and study of the Qur'an. They explain the importance of approaching the Sacred Book as Muslims and describe the ethics of how it should be recited, such as purification or performing ablutions and covering the aura, which differs for men and women. This study shows that even in predominantly Muslim societies, approaching the Qur'an remains a challenge. This raises the question of what we can expect for the community of Latin converts living in a non-Islamic context.

Another study focuses on the challenges faced by students when reciting the Qur'an among nursing university students in Indonesia (Supriyadi & Julia, 2019). Action research is used as a research design, in which teachers and researchers collaborate to identify problems among their students and suggest some solutions. The identified problems range from recognition of Arabic letters to the rules of recitation (*Tajweed*) and further toward understanding the message of the Qur'an. This research is relevant to our topic as it demonstrates that studying and learning Arabic, as well as reading, reciting, and understanding the Qur'an, is a challenge for any Muslim who is not a native Arabic speaker.

There is another study that analyses errors in Qur'an recitation among second-level of *tilawah*[5] students offered by the CELPAD (Center for Languages and Pre-University Academic Development) at the International Islamic University of Malaysia (IIUM) (Hassan & Zailaini, 2013). In this study, 20 students were asked to recite fragments from the Qur'an, and the researcher, who also served as an evaluator, identified and recorded the errors in their recitation according to established criteria within the rules of *Tajweed*. Developing techniques and skills in recitation is part of the program and credits required to complete professional studies. The author aimed to highlight the most common errors in recitation and present the findings to the academic department, with the intention of generating strategies to overcome these errors and improve the level of Qur'an recitation among the students, which is a requirement for anyone wishing to obtain a degree in Islamic studies and/or Arabic.

Figure 2.1. *IIUM Mosque Sultan Haji Ahmad Shah*

5 *Tilawah* is another term used for refering "recitation of the Qur'an".

My work doesn't include detecting errors in the recitation of the Qur'an among converts; it is not a study I would recommend conducting among the Latin American Muslim community because as a community we are still very new to the experience of approaching the Qur'an in Arabic. That type of assessment would drive converts away from the Qur'an rather than bring them closer, and the objective is to find the best way to approach and access the Qur'an in its original language. However, it is important to mention this study (Hassan & Zailaini, 2013) because, in other contexts, the study of the Qur'an serves other purposes beyond worship and praise, such as the aim of obtaining an academic degree.

Educational activities have two sides: one is learning, and the other is teaching. Regarding academic studies in the teaching of the Qur'an, I will first cite some studies about teaching in person and then those that are online and distance-based teaching. Research on in-person teaching includes the management of Qur'an recitation instruction among primary school teachers in Malaysia (Che Noh et al., 2019), where it was concluded that teachers need better preparation to teach the recitation of the Holy Book. There is also the example of a study in the United Kingdom on the teaching and learning of the Qur'an (Che Noh et al., 2014), which describes the teaching environment in the mosques in that particular country. It is interesting because the Muslims of the UK also are a minority with 4.4% of the population (PEW Research Center, 2012). One of the researchers' suggestions is that parents should dedicate more time to reinforcing Islamic education, including the study and recitation of the Qur'an.

An interesting study was found on effective techniques for memorizing the Qur'an in a school in Malaysia (Ariffin et al., 2013). The data collection methods included documentation, observation, and interviews. After two years (or a little more, depending on the memorization speed), 'graduated' students are able to recite the entire Qur'an in 15 hours, starting at 5:00 am and finishing at 10:00 pm, with breaks for water and food, taking about 30 minutes to read a *juzz* or part of the Qur'an. This method may be effective in a context where children and youth grow up with a strong Islamic tradition and identity centered around memorization, but it is not appropriate for the context of the community of converts in Latin America, specifically in Mexico and Colombia. On the other hand, I question the idea of reciting a *juzz* in 30 minutes and the entire Qur'an in 15 hours on the evaluation day, especially when a professional reciter like Mishary Al-Afasy takes just over an hour to recite a *juzz* with *Tarteel* and *Tajweed*, meaning with a melodious voice and following the rules of recitation.

Regarding online and distance education, research was conducted in Oman, which focuses on the online program for the recitation and memorization of the Qur'an. It is historically noted that in 1971, Sheikh Hilal bin Hamud al-Riyami designed the program 'The Seven-Fort Method for Memorizing the Holy Qur'an', which is also used by the national system of Qur'an schools in Senegal (Osborne, 2020). It was concluded that this teaching program is motivating for students and for memorizing the Qur'an in its entirety. 'Seven-Fort Method' is a software in which the student 'conquers' fortresses (or parts of a fortress) each time they memorize a section of the Qur'an. This study indicates that it is possible to seek cultural and contextually significant strategies, both digital and in-person, to motivate and assist students in reciting and memorizing the Holy Qur'an. The fortresses are part of the classical architecture of the Arabian Peninsula and the students of that region feel identified with that particular symbol.

Figure 2.2. *Architecture in the Arabian Peninsula. Arab Fortresses.*

An article was also found on the design of an online program for mass learning of Qur'an recitation (Wahid et al., 2019), which aims to respond to a large number of people who wish to learn to recite and memorize the Sacred Book. There are studies on digital engineering about the development of digital applications for the study of recitation, such as *Smartajweed* (Alagrami & Eljazzar, 2020) and *E-Hafiz*: an intelligent system to assist in recitation and memorization (Muhammad et al., 2012). Online programs and digital applications are known ways to learn the religion among converts in Latin America and it is important to explore this aspect.

Regarding the effects of reciting the Qur'an, whether through personal reading or listening to recitations, several studies were found. For example, one study investigated the regulation of anxiety levels in athletes (Mottaghi et al. 2011) and concluded that it is an effective, accessible, and medication-free method to reduce anxiety before competition. Another study found that mental and spiritual relaxation can be effectively induced through reciting and/or listening to the Qur'an (Khan et al. 2010). These results also emerged from a study comparing listening to the Qur'an versus music and its effects on brainwaves detected by electroencephalogram (Shekha et al. 2013). Additionally, another study examines the effects of reciting and listening to the Qur'an on the hearts of believers (Auwal et al., 2018), which is based on *hadith* and verses from the Qur'an, asserting that believers' faith increases when reciting and/or listening to the sacred text and that it is possible to experience inner peace. Identifying the effects of reciting the Qur'an is one of the objectives of this work.

2.2. Theoretical Framework

2.2.1. Adult Learning

Andragogy is the field focused on studying how adults engage in the teaching and learning process. The term was established by Malcolm Knowles in 1970 to refer the adult learning and to differentiate it from pedagogy and the learning of children. Andragogy assumes that adult learners have their own experiences, which are as valid and important as the knowledge and experience of the teacher or facilitator. It has six principles: the need to know, the self-concept, previous experience, readiness to learn, orientation to learning, and motivation to learn.

Andragogy proposes to focus on the student and establishes the difference between 'learning', which is an activity carried out by students, and 'teaching', which is an activity performed by teachers. Thus, education is an activity undertaken to produce changes in the knowledge, skills, and attitudes of individuals, groups, or communities. Learning can be viewed as a product (like a result or outcome), a process (which is the experience of learning itself and how that process occurs), or as a function (emphasizing the role of learning in feeling motivated, retaining information, or transferring knowledge).

How can adulthood be defined? In adult learning, the psychological definition of adulthood is the most appropriate, and in the context of Muslim converts, the decision to embrace Islam and make changes, as well as the engagement in learning about religion, is an exercise of their self-direction and self-assessment capabilities. Adults learn differently than children because they have established mental frameworks, experiences, and prior knowledge that can be useful or not, which can be integrated or discarded with the acquisition of new knowledge. However, being an adult also has negative effects; mental habits, tendencies, and biases can form, closing the mind to new learning, fresh ideas, and alternative ways of thinking (Knowles, 2001).

In the context of converts to Islam, the decision to embrace the faith and make changes in their lives and to engage in religious learning, is an exercise of their self-direction and self-assessment abilities as adults.

Women who convert to Islam in Mexico and Colombia are adults with the capacity to make decisions about their lives, able to self-direct their learning goals and objectives. From a psychological perspective, adulthood is characterized by a self-concept of being responsible for one's own life, having the power to make decisions in personal, professional, economic, and political matters. This capacity for self-direction is crucial. During the learning process, psychological adulthood is the most significant; the process of developing a self-concept and self-direction begins early and progressively increases alongside biological maturity, as individuals start to take their place as adults and take responsibility for their decisions and actions (Knowles, 2001). (See diagram 2.1).

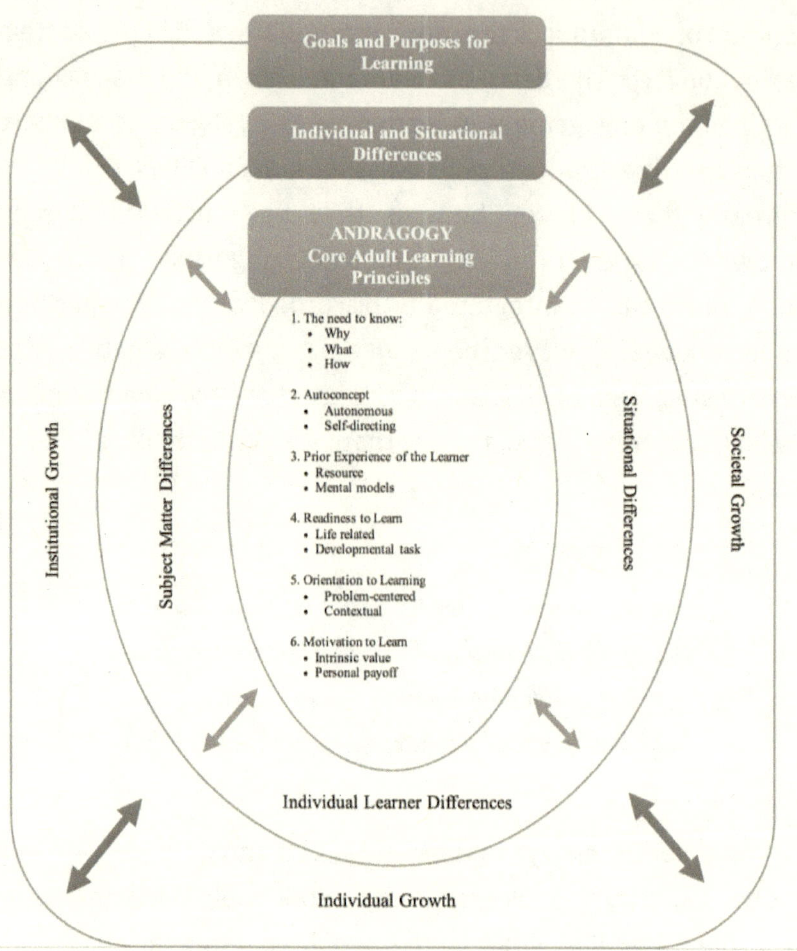

Figure 2.3. *Malcolm Knowles' Andragogical Model (1970)*

2.2.2. Intrinsic Motivation

Cook and Artino (2016) define motivation as a process aimed to achieve goals, where various activities and initiatives are initiated and sustained until accomplished. Motivation involves movement, energy, direction, the reason for behavior, defining 'what is done' and answering, 'why it is done' (Ryan & Deci, 2000). Motivation is classified into two types based on the factors that trigger it: intrinsic motivation is based on challenges, curiosity, imagination, and desire, while extrinsic motivation is driven by rewards or fear of punishment (Ryan & Deci, 2000).

Active learning stimulates intrinsic motivation, which manifests when an individual 'wants' to learn or accomplish something due to their desire. It has also been studied in the context of 'curiosity', defined as the anticipation of rewarding information. Learning is perceived by individuals as inherently gratifying, eliminating the need for extrinsic rewards (Bruya & Tang, 2021). Adult learning relies on students' intrinsic motivation, such as satisfaction, personal growth, spirituality, self-esteem, self-confidence, skill or competence development, and improving the quality of life. These are more effective motivators for adult learning (Knowles, 2001). This research investigates the motivations that drive converts to embark on and persevere in their studies of Arabic and the recitation of the Qur'an.

2.2.3. Attention and Concentration

Learning also requires students to pay attention. What is the relationship between attention and intrinsic motivation? Attention is essential for learning, development, interpersonal relationships, health, and daily life. Attention is the direction of mental activity and the preservation of this selected activity, while concentration means immersion in the given activity and distraction from everything else (Bruya & Tang, 2021). There are two types of attention: involuntary and voluntary. When the direction and concentration are linked to emotions and stimuli from the environment, requiring no effort and being exclusively perceptual sources, it is referred to as 'involuntary attention'. Conversely, if the direction and focus are selective and conscious, it is termed 'voluntary attention', which is aimed to achieve a goal and requires one or several types of effort (Bruya & Tang, 2021).

Bruya and Tang (2021) introduce a third type, the 'fluid attention', which is directed toward specific goals and is selective, not requiring effort and being drawn to the source. This type is characterized by the motivational component and is also referred to as 'post-voluntary attention'. When learning a new activity, the individual needs to use voluntary motivation until mastering that activity. At that point, fluid attention is deployed. They propose that learning is achieved through 'interesting' activities or those that generate 'curiosity', producing dopamine in the brain and activating voluntary attention for learning. Once a certain level of skill in the new task or knowledge is attained, along with emotional control, management of the fear of making mistakes, nervousness, and anxiety, as well as the development of self-assurance and confidence, fluid attention is then activated (Bruya & Tang, 2021).

Attention and concentration in adult learning activities largely depend on the individuals themselves. However, this can be achieved by considering the andragogical teaching model (Knowles, 2001) and addressing the needs of adults, such as understanding the reasons for learning, the benefits, costs, efforts, and viewing them as self-directed individuals. This approach helps foster independent, self-directed learners. To understand the experience and learning process of converts to Islam, it is crucial to comprehend the type of attention that is deployed in learning Arabic and reciting the Qur'an, as well as what occurs when no form of attention is present.

2.2.4. Emotion Regulation

An adult is defined as someone capable of self-direction, self-evaluation, and self-control. However, what happens when we are unable to regulate our emotions? Religious conversion brings about various internal and external changes (Mondragón, 2023) that can impact an individual's emotions. The lack of emotional regulation affects attention and concentration, which in turn impacts learning in adults (Wadlinger & Isaacowitz, 2011). This could pose a challenge for converts to Islam. Training attention and concentration can serve as an important regulator of emotions, and attentional regulation can also be developed through practice and repetitions (Perry & Winfrey, 2021; Wadlinger & Isaacowitz, 2011).

2.3. Methodology

The design of this research is qualitative; it is exploratory and falls within the category of action research. This involves exploring a practical problem, where researchers and participants collaborate to identify causes with the aim of developing a solution to the problem and contributing to the social group (Berg, 2001; Leavy, 2017). Action research encompasses principles of participation and reflection (Berg, 2001). This research design is relevant because it aims to explore the barriers to access our sacred text, the Qur'an, alongside the community of Latin Muslim converts from Mexico and Colombia. The primary barrier is language, which hinders our connection to the Qur'an. The goal is to encourage more Spanish-speaking Muslim converts to engage with and access the Qur'an for reading, recitation, study, and memorization.

Muslims in Mexico and Colombia make up less than 1% of the total population in both countries (PEW Research Center, 2012). Some of them are immigrants from various Muslim countries, while another portion consists of Mexicans and Colombians who have converted to Islam, the majority of whom are women. The sample is non-probabilistic and not representative of the community; a deliberate sample was used. In this case, the researcher utilizes her own experience and contacts to reach a specific group of individuals who can respond to the interview and help meet the project's objectives. The researcher ensured that the participants met specific requirements: Muslim women converts with experience in learning the Arabic language and the rules of Qur'anic recitation. A total of eight women converts to Islam were interviewed, each with different life experiences and academic levels, and their places of origin are Mexico or Colombia. Personal codes were created for each participant to ensure anonymity and confidentiality. (See table 2.2).

Code	***Age***	***Origin***	***Marital status***	***Time of conversion***	***Education level***	***Languages***
RM-1-MX	34	Mexico	married	2011	Bachelor	Spanish English Arabic
SU-2-MX	35	Mexico	divorce	2004	High School	Spanish English
MC-3-MX	41	Mexico	married	2013	Technical degree Tailoring	Spanish
SV-4-MX	30	Mexico	married	2013	Bachelor	Spanish English

Code	*Age*	*Origin*	*Marital status*	*Time of conversion*	*Education level*	*Languages*
GC-5-MX	50	Mexico	married	1998	*Ijazza- Tajweed*	Spanish English Arabic
KA-6-CL	36	Colombia	married	2012	Master	Spanish English Arabic Latin
LH-7-CL	41	Colombia	married	2001	Master	Spanish English Arabic Turkish

Code	*Age*	*Origin*	*Marital status*	*Time of conversion*	*Education level*	*Languages*
LI-8-CL	66	Colombia	widow	1980	Bachelor	Spanish English German Egyptian Arabic Qur'anic Arabic

Table 2.2. *Participants' Demographics*

In-depth interviews were used to understand the participants' experiences, challenges, problems, and suggestions (Flick, 2009; Patton, 2002). Data collection took place via WhatsApp between June and July 2022. The results were subsequently presented to the participants in May 2024, who confirmed the findings. Data collection was conducted through digital platforms, as the internet has the capacity to connect people situated in different geographical locations. Data management was done using Atlas.ti 8 to categorize responses by codes, and Word was later used for further analysis.

The researcher identifies as a facilitator and part of the community being studied. According to Berg (2001), in action research, the researcher is not an external observer but is aware of the potential impact of the intervention or study and its capacity for change. Most action research aims to study something to change it or improve it (Leavy, 2017). The researcher collaborates with his area of expertise when participants need assistance. The researcher's approach is more holistic, encompassing various dimensions and aspects that may influence participants (including technological, social, economic, and political factors) while maintaining an interpersonal relationship with each individual (Berg, 2001).

The strategies that the researcher used to gain reliability included conducting thematic analysis: (1) familiarizing oneself with the data, (2) generating initial codes based on the research questions, (3) searching for recurring themes and identifying particularities, (4) reviewing themes according to data coding and identifying deficiencies, (5) defining and naming themes, and (6) producing the report that will present the patterns in the responses (Nowell et al., 2017).

Subsequently, the data were verified with the participants, and the findings were presented to them, which is part of the procedures in action research design. External professional reviews were conducted to assess the objectives in two dimensions: first, in terms of theoretical-methodological technicalities with the help of Dr. Arely Medina from the University of Guadalajara well known for her work on research about Islam in Latin America (Medina, 2012, 2017, 2018, 2019, 2023), and second, for theological and religious issues exclusive to Islam with the Ustadh Omar Weston, well known Muslim convert living in Mexico and recognized as one of the pioneers in institutionalizing Islam in Mexico (Pastor, 2015). Both types of reviews aimed to avoid the researcher's personal bias. Finally, reflection on the action of researching (Schön, 1998) was applied at various stages of the research.

Chapter 3

Findings. The Journey of the Qur'an to Conversion

3.1. Brief Stories of the Participants' Conversion

The short conversion stories of the participants are presented to understand their backgrounds. They answered two questions: how did they know about Islam? and what motivated their conversion? (See table 3.1).

Code	*How did she know about Islam?*	*Motivation for Conversion*
RM-1-MX	Subject on the Middle East class at the university where she began her Arabic studies without being a Muslim.	A slow and gradual process that began with university studies and the learning of Arabic. I gradually changed, adopting Islamic practices. one day, I made my *shahada*, which came naturally, and continued to make changes little by little.

Code	*How did she know about Islam?*	*Motivation for Conversion*
SU-2-MX	Books of poetry at the CCH (College of Sciences and Humanities) at UNAM. One book in particular about Arab aesthetic thought that led her to the Qur'an.	Search for the truth: at five years old, she wore a headscarf and fasted; she already knew a little about Islam. What she read about Islam was similar to what she had read in the Bible, and when she read about Muhammad (saw), her heart was certain that Islam was what she needed.
MC-3-MX	Through internet searches about abused Muslim women, followed by contact on Facebook.	She was looking for information about the mistreatment of women in Islam, but instead, she found the rights of women and their importance in Islam. She began to read more and identified increasingly with what she read. Eventually, after seeing the saints and idols as false, she decided to destroy them and convert to Islam.

Code	*How did she know about Islam?*	*Motivation for Conversion*
SV-4-MX	For a Muslim contact or friend on Facebook and searching on the internet.	It was the Qur'an (translated into Spanish) that answered the questions I had after reading and studying the Bible as a Christian.
GC-5-MX	Marriage Start practicing after a big loss.	She was already living with a Muslim, but she didn't practice because she didn't have a role model to learn from. Through the loss of a daughter, she felt depressed and lost, and she began to turn to Allah (swt) for refuge and to find peace.
KA-6-CL	For a colleague who converted to Islam, after a time, she got married to him.	Monotheism was logical for her.
LH-7-CL	She met a Muslim woman while studying abroad.	I found a pure spirituality in Islam. I really liked how Muslim women dressed; they seemed very feminine to me. I discovered the monotheism I had been searching for.

Code	*How did she know about Islam?*	*Motivation for Conversion*
LI-8-CL	Information in high school. Contact with Muslims at university, and I would ask them about Islam.	Search for the truth. I conducted a comparative study of Catholicism and Islam, and I chose Islam. The concept of *tawhid* became very clear to me and brought me great peace in dispelling the myth of the Trinity.

Table 3.1. *Brief Stories of Participants' Conversion*

3.2. Perspective On Learning Arabic and *Tajweed*

Response to Research Question No. 1: *What is the perspective of convert Muslim women on the Islamic tradition of learning to read Arabic and reciting the Qur'an melodiously?* Learning Arabic and reciting the Qur'an is an Islamic tradition; it is Sunnah and an obligation for all Muslims (Hosein, 2020). This tradition originates from the pre-Islamic era and became part of the revelation of the Qur'an (Alkhateeb, 2014). It is considered Sunnah because it reflects how the word of Allah (swt) was revealed to the Prophet Muhammad (saw), and it is obligatory for Muslims to perform at least the five daily prayers, during which they must recite at least *Surah Al Fatiha*.

The findings indicate that this tradition doesn't pass automatically on to convert Muslim women in Mexico and Colombia. There is a process comprised of experiences, learning, and decisions that ultimately lead them to embark on the journey from their conversion to Islam, to access the Qur'an in its original language. I see these journeys as a labyrinth with various beginnings and different paths, but a common end: the access to the Qur'an. The objectives of this study don't include the speed of learning or the time taken to walk the path, nor does it matter the level of fluency in recitation, the number of *suras* memorized, or the Arabic knowledge each participant possesses. What is being observed is the trajectory—the ups and downs, the challenges, difficulties, and how to overcome them; that is, the process of learning.

By analyzing the participants' responses, I found that they express confusion and a total lack of understanding about what it means to access the Qur'an in its original language, especially at the time of their conversion or at the beginning of their learning journey. Only one of the eight participants mentioned an initial desire to learn Arabic in order to access the original sacred text, as translations of other sacred writings (e.g., the Old and New Testaments, i.e., the Bible) which did not seem genuine to her (LI-8-CL).

The participants mentioned that they were unaware of what was necessary to learn to recite the Qur'an or even ignored the importance of accessing the Qur'an in its original language or how to do so. Two testimonies are cited as evidence:

> "The truth is that it was not a conscious decision (starting the studies of Qur'an). I do remember that it was my desire to be able to recite the Qur'an in its original language, but I had no guidance. I was taking an Arabic course, starting one book, then another, but I wasn't aware that there are rules for reciting the Qur'an, that there are even types of recitation, that there are styles of recitation. I don't know how to explain it; I wasn't aware of all of these. I thought you just read the letters and no more. So, *Subhan Allah*, it was Allah (swt) who guided me, because I remember that I

made a *dua* (supplication), and I really wanted to learn to recite the Qur'an in its language and to recite it well, but I didn't know how, I wasn't aware." (SV-4-MC)

"I started studying in the same year I converted to Islam. I felt a bit of confusion; the truth is, I had just converted, and everything was new to me. I didn't even know that there were 'Islamic sciences'; I didn't know anything at all. Honestly, I was very new; it was confusing. But it wasn't that I had consciously decided to study *Tajweed* or *Tafseer* or all those things. I went to study in Egypt with my husband, and there we studied all that as part of the curriculum in the institute; it wasn't something I had sought out, honestly." (KA-6-CL)

Two of the participants started Arabic classes before embracing Islam (RM-1-MX and LI-8-CL), one for professional reasons (RM-1-MX) and the other, out of interest in reading a sacred text in its original language (LI-8-CL). Three participants had their first exposure with the help of Pakistani Muslim neighbors; these were informal, intermittent classes, but they consider it an important initial step toward approaching Arabic letters (MC-3-MX, SV-4-MX, and GC-5-MX). One participant started learning Arabic at the time of her conversion in the UK because she was in contact with Muslim women (LH-7-CL).

During their initial approach to classes, the participants mentioned various emotions: ignorance, confusion, nervousness ranging from moderate to extreme, anxiety, difficulty. However, one participant mentioned having positive feelings, such as a sense of peace, happiness, ease, interest, and motivation, mostly at the beginning of the studies (LH-7-CL). The participants mentioned experiencing more than one emotion simultaneously during their first encounters with Arabic studies and recitation to access the Qur'an.

Once the participants understood what it means to access the Qur'an in its original language, they began to make their own learning decisions. They started to see difficulties as challenges and set achievable goals for themselves. For example, five out of the eight participants mentioned having incorrectly memorized some *suras* they learned through audio, transliterations, or reading, and they decided to correct them (RM-1-MX, SU-2-MX, MC-3-MX, and SV-4-MX). Another participant decided to enroll her children in an Islamic institute where she also memorized small *suras* and learned the basic memorization techniques (GC-5-MX). One participant, along with her Muslim husband, made a conscious decision to study *Tafseer* and memorize *juzz amma* (the last part of the Qur'an that begins with *Surah* No. 78, titled *An-Naba'*) with *Tajweed* (rules of recitation), and that study lasted several years (LI-8-CL).

3.3. Learning Process of the Participants

Response to question No. 2: *What is the experience of female converts to Islam, particularly in Mexico and Colombia, in approaching the Qur'an in Arabic to read, understand, and recite it?*

To answer this question, the following aspects will be considered as part of the learning experience of Arabic and *Tajweed* among female converts to Islam: opportunities for study abroad or in their home country, online or in-person learning modalities, the effect of the COVID-19 pandemic, accessibility of material resources, and costs.

Experiences abroad, whether for studies, marriage, or travel, have shaped their journey of learning Arabic and *Tajweed*. Five women have studied abroad, and three have remained in their home countries. All have experienced online and in-person classes to varying degrees. Two of the participants are in constant mobility due to family and health reasons, which impacts their learning journey.

The women who have had the experience of living and studying abroad mentioned that daily interaction with Arabic speakers has significantly strengthened their learning of Arabic (RM-1-MX, GC-5-MX, KA-6-CL, LH-7-CL, and LI-8-CL). They acknowledge the difference between the Egyptian dialect and Qur'anic Arabic; five participants learned Egyptian Arabic for everyday communication and understand the Qur'an according to their level of knowledge of classical and Qur'anic Arabic (see table 3.2 to observe the demographics of those who have had study experiences abroad). However, the women who remained in their home countries and seek online Arabic classes to understand the Qur'an report progress in their understanding of the Book, perhaps not necessarily for communicative purposes (SU-2-MX, MC-3-MX, and SV-4-MX). Although the learning process is slow, they find it meaningful. The following testimonies are presented as evidence:

> *Participant with experience abroad:* "It's important to remember that you don't need to learn Arabic as a means of social communication. The basic sciences[6] of the Qur'an can be learned without having to speak Arabic. An example is Indonesian reciters who have memorized the Qur'an without speaking Arabic. I've also seen thousands of participants in the DREAM program of *Al Bayyina* Institute, most of whom are not Arabs, and how they have learned *nahw* (grammar), *sarf* (morphology), and *balagha* from

6 It is common to hear Muslims talk about "sciences" of Islam or the Qur'an. The word "science" in this context should not be understood in the same way as Western science; it refers to the "knowledge" of the Qur'an.

explanations in English, which is not their native language either. *Subhan Allah.*" (LI-8-CL)

Participant who has remained in her home country: "I consider having more fluency to be an important achievement because I read slowly, but I don't get stuck as much anymore. So, it is an accomplishment, but I still want to improve, not necessarily to go faster, but to avoid getting stuck or making mistakes in reading, and to make it more fluid." (SV-4-MX)

Code	***Origin***	***Places where she lived or studied***	***Current residency***
RM-1-MX	Mexico	Egypt United Arab Emirates	United Arab Emirates
SU-2-MX	Mexico	Mexico	Mexico
MC-3-MX	Mexico	Mexico	Mexico
SV-4-MX	Mexico	Mexico	Mexico
GC-5-MX	Mexico	United States Egypt	United States Constant mobility
KA-6-CL	Colombia	Egypt	Colombia

Code	*Origin*	*Places where she lived or studied*	*Current residency*
LH-7-CL	Colombia	England Egypt Malaysia Turkey	Turkey
LI-8-CL	Colombia	England Germany Egypt Saudi Arabia	Colombia Constant mobility

Table 3.2. *Study Experience: Local or Abroad*

It is understood that every learning activity is a process of seeking information and requires physical and mental effort (Mondragón, 2023), as well as material and financial resources. Accessibility to learning the Qur'an and Arabic is considered with the following characteristics: (1) if it is in-person, factors like distance, means of transportation, travel time, and costs are considered, and (2) if it is online, whether they have the necessary digital devices, a stable internet connection, and the costs of the courses. All eight participants have had access to free online classes, which implies an internet connection and at least one device they can use to access the class. One of them has paid for an online course on Qur'anic Arabic (LI-8-CL). Two Mexican participants have focused their learning through the online modality because it is the only available option, as they do not have a nearby Islamic community and even less access to in-person teachers (SU-2-MX and SV-3-MX). This involves making the effort late at night or early in the morning due to different time zones. One of them mentioned having problems with the internet connection because the geographical area where she lives is rural.

Five of the participants have had the opportunity to study abroad: one with financial aid (KA-6-CL), two due to marriage and living in Arab countries (RM-1-MX and LI-8-CL), and two other women with their own resources and their spouses (GC-5-MX and LH-7-CL). One of the participants has access to in-person classes at the local mosque in Mexico, where she attends irregularly due to the distance and travel time within Mexico City. She opts to take the class online when she cannot attend in person (MC-3-MX).

Data collection took place shortly after the end of the COVID-19 pandemic isolation, and the fear of going out and socializing with others was still present. In this study, it is relevant to mention the participants' experiences, as some of them began online classes during the isolation period. One of the participants mentioned having mental health issues and completely stopped reciting the Qur'an and studying Arabic (RM-1-MX). For five participants, it was an opportunity to start or resume their studies with more intensity (SU-2-MX, MC-3-MX, SV-4-MX, GC-5-MX, and LI-8-CL) because they mentioned that, as a result of being required to stay home, many online courses became available, and they were able to dedicate time to them. By being consistent and disciplined, they managed to make progress during the isolation period. The following testimony is evidence of a positive effect of the COVID-19 isolation:

> "*Alhamdulillah*, in the middle of the quarantine, I started taking the intensive DREAM course on Qur'anic Arabic. The course has been, and still is to this day, my source of

motivation to connect with the Qur'an on a deeper level, and each day I am more amazed by this great miracle." (LI-8-CL)

"What the pandemic brought were a lot of students and children as well (to the online courses we offer at the As Sabeel Institute). Of course, the classes are intermittent, and only a small percentage continue (mostly with longer and bigger goals). The pandemic also allowed sisters living in various parts of the world to connect, and we were all in different time zones. I had students from all continents." (GC-5-MX)

The participants mentioned that online *Tajweed* classes have some disadvantages, starting with the fact that the visual aspect is important in the learning process. Additionally, one of them mentions the challenge of following an online class. The following testimonies serve as evidence:

"The pandemic affected because I stopped teaching in-person classes. Face-to-face classes are the best because you are seeing the person, you are hearing them directly. When you hear someone through a microphone or any audio device, it's very different because you are not seeing the person reciting directly. And here, for example, in online classes, even though we ask them to turn on their cameras, not all of them are willing to do so, and it's also hard to properly detect how they are reading since you can't see them directly." (GC-5-MX)

"Last year, during an intensive course to memorize *Surah Al-Mulk*, each student recited an *ayah*, and the teacher would correct each one. She would say, 'Behind the microphone, you should keep repeating the *ayah* until you memorize it,' and I tried to do that. But she also told us, 'Watch the corrections of your classmates so that you don't make the same mistakes.' I tried to do that as well. As the class progressed, because there were so many of us, the end of the session approached, and we still hadn't finished the *Surah*, so the teacher rushed us. Then the teacher would take a turn, reciting extremely fast, which seemed a bit contradictory to me because I wasn't hearing the timings she had pointed out in her own recitation, and that caused more stress. I ended up focusing only on practicing the *ayah* I was going to read, trying to read it as fast as possible. When it was my turn, I was extremely nervous, and the teacher corrected me a lot. In the end, I didn't memorize anything at all." (SV-4-MX)

According to the mentioned testimonies, it is better to have face-to-face practice of vocal exercises, training, and finding the articulation points for Arabic letters rather than online. It is important for the learner to be able to see the teacher's mouth movements in order to produce the correct sounds or for the teacher to see the student to correct them. On the other hand, online group classes have their own format and characteristics, and a traditional in-person group class cannot be directly transferred to an online format as it is. Teachers need to find the proper ways to teach the *Tajweed* technique using the online format because, for the majority of Muslim converts living in non-Muslim countries, the classes of *Tajweed* and Arabic language it is mostly online.

3.4. The Journey from the Qur'an to the Religious Conversion

Regardless the first very motivation to pronounce *shahada* or the testimony of faith, the Qur'an and its message of the oneness of Allah (swt) was understand by the participants early or later on their path to conversion and it was the main reasons why the participants embarked on their learning journey towards the Arabic language to access the Qur'an. We could say that the participants' learning journeys move from a translation of the Qur'an to the religious conversion, and then go back to the Qur'an in its original language, where they rediscover it and connect with the Holy Book in the language in which it was revealed.

The woman's learning journeys move from a translation of the Qur'an to the religious conversion, and then go back to the Qur'an in its original language, where they rediscover it and connect with the Holy Book in the language in which it was revealed.

It's not the norm, but many female Muslim converts confuse the Qur'an with its translation, and this is what this research is about: it is necessary to distinguish one from the other to give each its proper place. Generally, converts to Islam have their first encounter with the Qur'an through translations in their native language. On this regard, the Qur'an has been fully translated into at least 47 different languages, and partially into at least 114 languages (Mossad, 2017), although not all translations are accredited or reliable (Embarek, 2000; Epalza, 2003; García, 2013; Pedraza, 2015). Ideally, translations of the Qur'an should be done with the goal of making it accessible to as many people as possible, including those with visual, auditory, speech, or neurodivergent challenges.

Translations into various languages can have a significant impact on the reader's life, influencing their decisions, actions, and even transforming aspects of their entire lifestyle. One of the most important and profound changes is the conversion to Islam, which involves a shift in religious identity (García, 2014; Medina, 2012; Mondragón, 2023). The topic of deconstruction and reconstruction of identity has been studied in works related to conversion to Islam (Al-Qwidi, 2002; Cañas Cuevas, 2015; Mansson, 2006; Medina, 2012; Mondragón, 2023; Vroon-Najem, 2014). Reading a translation is an 'experimental' action among converts, but the decisions and actions that follow—such as implementing daily prayers or fasting during the month of Ramadan—are classified as decisive actions and acts of commitment (to the religion, to Allah swt, etc.) (Al-Qwidi, 2002).

The evidence from this study also shows that the participants enter a process of deconstruction and reconstruction of identity through reading a translation of the Qur'an. Even being exposed to information about Islam is enough for them to decide to convert to Islam. The evidence indicates that the Muslim female converts who participated in the interviews enter a process of strengthening their religious identity when they begin their learning journey with the goal of accessing the Qur'an in its original language (see diagram 3.3).

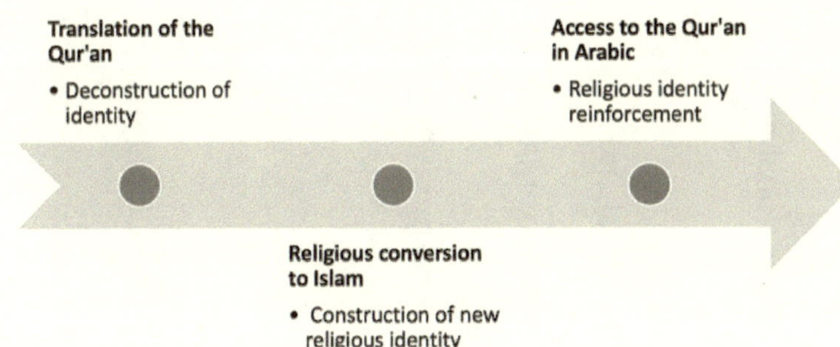

Figure 3.3. *Deconstruction, Construction, and Reinforcement of Religious Identity.*

It is interesting to pay attention to the moment when the participants began their studies of Arabic and *Tajweed*. Two of them started before their conversion to Islam (RM-1-MX and LI-8-CL), two began at the same time as their conversion (KA-6-CL and LH-7-CL), and the rest started years after their conversion (SU-2-MX, MC-3-MX, SV-4-MX, and GC-5-MX). This allows us to conclude that the starting point of the learning journey is different for each person and depends on two factors: the circumstances and situations the person is experiencing, and secondly, the initial motivations behind the decision to start studying. (See table 3.4).

Time of initiation	*Code*	*Testimony*	*Initial motivation*
Before conversion to Islam	RM-1-MX	I started to write my bachelor thesis about Muslim women.	Professional reason.
	LI-8-CL	I wanted to read a Holy Scripture in its original language. I started to learn Arabic to understand the Qur'an.	Personal and Religious reasons.
At the same time of conversion to Islam	KA-6-CL	I didn't know exactly why I had to study Arabic and Qur'an. I started because they gave me financial aid to study in Egypt; it was an opportunity to study abroad.	Opportunity to study abroad
	LH-7-CL	Out of curiosity, it was interesting to see lines above mean A, lines below mean E.	Personal interest. Curiosity

Time of initiation	*Code*	*Testimony*	*Initial motivation*
After conversion to Islam	SU-2-MX	The need to guide and teach my son.	To share knowledge
	MC-3-MX	To read the Qur'an.	Personal and Religious reasons.
	SV-4-MX	I didn't quite understand why at first. Then I started with the letters, without giving them much importance, and later I restarted out of a sense of guilt for not having appreciated my first teacher. I passed from teacher to teacher without grasping the importance of learning Arabic and the Qur'an. May Allah (swt) guide me to understand how important it is for a Muslim to access the Qur'an in Arabic.	Confusion Sense of guilt Religious reason

Time of initiation	*Code*	*Testimony*	*Initial motivation*
After conversion to Islam	GC-5-MX	I wanted to teach my children to communicate in Arabic. I need to alleviate the effects of traumatic events. For reciting and understanding the Qur'an because it is the word of Allah (swt).	Communication Psychological Personal and Religious reasons.

Table 3.4. *Initial motivation to study Qur'an and Arabic*

However, the participants' motivations changed according to the experiences and situations they faced. The context in which they were raised, and the particular situation and motivation for conversion to Islam, are factors that influenced their learning. The motivations evolve through the time and at the moment of conducting the interviews, they all identified that their current motivation for studying Arabic and *Tajweed* is to access the Holy Qur'an. This includes connecting with the Holy Book, reciting it, understanding what it says word-by-word, understanding its interpretation, comprehending its meanings through Arabic grammar, sharing the knowledge with others, whether with their children or other converts, gaining fluency in reciting it, and memorizing as much as possible. See table 3.5 for a summary of the evolution of learning motivations.

Time of initiation	*Code*	*Initial motivation*	*2nd Motivation*	*3rd Motivation (Current)*
Before conversion to Islam	RM-1-MX	Professional reason.	Marriage Cultural reason Communication purposes	To understand the Qur'an. Recite it constantly.
	LI-8-CL	Personal and Religious reasons.	Communication purposes Religious	To understand the Qur'an. Seek connection with the Qur'an through recitation, meaning, and grammar.

Time of initiation	***Code***	***Initial motivation***	***2nd Motivation***	***3rd Motivation (Current)***
At the same time of conversion to Islam	KA-6-CL	Confusion Opportunity to study abroad	Continue with the studies to complete the program	To understand the Qur'an through Arabic grammar.
	LH-7-CL	Personal interest. Curiosity	To understand the Qur'an.	To recite it To understand the Qur'an. Interpretation *Tafseer*, meaning word-by-word.

Time of initiation	*Code*	*Initial motivation*	*2nd Motivation*	*3rd Motivation (Current)*
After conversion to Islam	SU-2-MX	To share	To share the knowledge	To understand the Qur'an. To share the knowledge.
	MC-3-MX	Personal and Religious reasons.	To understand the Qur'an.	To understand the Qur'an. Memorize it
	SV-4-MX	Confusion Sense of guilt Religious reason	Communication purposes with the teachers	To understand the Qur'an. Get fluency in recitation Memorize it

Time of initiation	*Code*	*Initial motivation*	*2nd Motivation*	*3rd Motivation (Current)*
After conversion to Islam	GC-5-MX	Psychological purposes Communication Personal and Religious reasons.	To share the knowledge To find guidance in life	To understand the Qur'an. To pray correctly and recite it fluently. To share the knowledge Memorize it Find guidance

Table 3.5. *Evolution of learning motivations*

Listening to reciters through audio is a common practice for all participants before, during, and after their conversion to Islam, as well as accessing the meanings through translations, both in Spanish and English. Four participants memorized some *suras* incorrectly by learning them through audio or transliterations and had to relearn the *suras* or *ayaat* to correct their pronunciation and memorization. I observe that the beginning is experimental; however, once there is an understanding of the importance and awareness of what studying Arabic and *Tajweed* entails, this is when the converts make decisions and seek study options to guide their learning. In all cases, whether in-person or online, this requires self-directed and personal efforts on practicing, studying, reading, recitation, repetition, memorization, etc., in addition to the teacher-led class.

The above has shown the role of Qur'anic translations and the evolution of learning motivations among the participants. Through this process, the learning journey to access the Qur'an can be seen as involving the deconstruction, construction, and reinforcement of religious identity. The conclusion is that the starting points for each woman's studies are different, depending on her context, personal situation, and the opportunities presented to her. The conscious decision to learn Arabic and *Tajweed* to access the Qur'an developed over the time. Initially, there is a lack of knowledge and confusion about what it means to recite or study the Qur'an.

3.5. Challenges and Difficulties

Response to question No. 3: *What challenges and difficulties do they face in this task?* To answer this question, I made a classification based on the participants' responses. It is necessary to present a brief definition of what a challenge, an obstacle, and frustration are. According to the Royal Spanish Academy (RAE), a *challenge* is a difficult objective or task to carry out, which therefore constitutes a stimulus and a trial for the person facing it. An *obstacle* in learning refers to difficulties or elements that arise through the interaction between the learner and the context, limiting access to new knowledge and learning opportunities (Mujica-Sequera, 2015). On the other hand, an emotional *obstacle* is a difficulty in managing feelings of helplessness, suffering, and anxiety, manifesting as fear of failure, lack of self-confidence, or a tendency to self-sabotage (Fernández-Alcántara et al., 2013; Mujica-Sequera, 2015). *Frustration* is defined as an unpleasant emotion that arises when a person cannot achieve something important to them, despite the physical, mental, and emotional efforts, attitudes, and time invested to set goal or objective. This could result in the cancellation of the objective and the abandonment of goals (DGDH Facultad de Psicología, 2022).

The participants reported the existence of individual and community challenges. Individual challenges include letter pronunciation, applying and remembering the rules of recitation or *Tajweed*, memorization (see table 3.6), making significant cognitive efforts, finding time to attend classes and study, and correcting incorrect memorization. Community challenges include gender segregation, especially in communities where Muslims are a minority, the ignorance of etiquette for learning and teaching, the individualistic approach to learning, reading only transliterations, the use of online classes that mimic traditional in-person formats, and individuals trying to multitask. These situations shared by the participants are considered as challenges that, with effort and dedication, they can overcome, whether on an individual or community level.

Pronunciation Challenges and Recitation Technique		
Letter identification	ك ق ض ظ ذ د ز س ص ن ل	ه خ ح ت ط غ ع
Letter pronunciation	ح خ غ ق ص ض	ط ظ ث
Interchange and confusion of letters within words.	1. Confusion:	2. Correct:
	Bisminahi *Bismila-í*	Bismillahi بسم الله
	Alhamduniná	*Alhamdulillah* الحمدلله
	Salan aleikun	*Salam Aleikum* السلام عليكم

Pronunciation Challenges and Recitation Technique	
Tajweed **rules**	*Lam Shamsiya* *Lam Qamariya* Letters with *sukun* and *shadda*. Breath control for elongation Rules of *idgham shafawi*. Rules of *nun* and *mim* Pronunciation of *Gunnah*. Rules of *ikhfa*: get the *gunnah* without getting the complete sound of *mim* and *nun*.
Memorization (of Qur'an means...)	A challenge (RM-1-MX, SU-2-MX, SV-4-MX, LH-7-CL) A wish (MC-3-MX) A goal (GC-5-MX, LI-8-CL). Frustration (KA-6-CL)

Table 3.6. *Pronunciation Challenges and Recitation Techniques*

The obstacles in learning that they reported include: family opposition to their conversion, economic situations, internet failures, connection and technology issues, and geographical distances. The emotional obstacles they mentioned were a lack of motivation and mental barriers such as 'I can't,' feelings of depression, setting overly high goals that are difficult to achieve, extreme mental exhaustion, feelings of shame, loneliness, overwhelm, worry, nervousness, stress, and fear during classes. A lack of interest in learning, studying, and reading in general is also a community obstacle.

The frustrations they mentioned include the real situation of Latin Muslim women, with several being single mothers who work or daughters whose parents prevent them from studying. This leads to little attendance or no registration at all into the lessons, whether in-person or online, and consequently results in interrupted studies, stagnation, or even dropout. They also reported a lack of empathy from Arab teachers, whether in-person or online. The absence of in-person *Tajweed* courses results in unfinished goals and study plans incomplete. The cancellation of both online and in-person classes, an overload of instructions that are difficult to follow, and when the teacher asks students to repeat without properly indicating where the error lies, were also sources of frustration. Additionally, losing or lowering their level of Arabic or recitation due to not practicing regularly was another significant issue.

The taboos surrounding the Qur'an are a source of frustration for them. These taboos create obstacles in learning and frustration among the participants, such as:

1. Only Arab teachers can teach.
2. It's wrong for a Mexican or Colombian mother, to teach the Qur'an or Arabic to her children.
3. Only Arabs can pronounce the letters correctly, and Latinos cannot.
4. Teaching must be done according to the student's ability without correcting their mistakes.
5. The Qur'an is so sacred that it shouldn't be touched.

6. It's a sin to make a mistake in the pronunciation of letters or words in the Qur'an.

7. Women cannot touch, recite, or look at the Qur'an during menstruation or postpartum periods.

8. Women cannot recite in public, including in mixed-gender classes.

Taboos are addressed with information. Accurate and on-time information allows us to eliminate or reinforce ideas to make the best decisions. It is important to dedicate time to review what the Qur'an says, what the *Sunnah* says (tradition of the Prophet Muhammad saw), and to consider the schools of Islamic jurisprudence, while also taking into account the context of the convert Muslim. This is the methodology I personally identify with and have learned throughout my own journey of converting to Islam and learning about the religion. Each topic should be reviewed through these sources, and then the most suitable decision for the student can be made. Learning and reciting the Qur'an is a very personal and individual task, but it has a community impact. Each person should make his or her own decisions on how and when to access the Holy Qur'an, whether for recitation, understanding its meanings, or studying it. Allah (swt) rewards those who approach the Qur'an for each letter they recite, as indicated by the following hadith:

> *"Whoever reads a letter from the Book of Allah (swt) will receive a reward. And each reward, Allah (swt) multiplies by 10. And I am not saying that Alif Lam Mim is a letter, but Alif is a letter, Lam is another, and Mim is another."* (Reported by At-Tirmidhi)

3.6. Positive Effects of Recitation and Study of Arabic

Response to question No. 4: *What are the positive effects of accessing the Qur'an in its original language?* To answer this question, two aspects are considered: first, what the Qur'an represents to the participants at the time of data collection; second, the achievements and positive effects they have experienced as a result of their studies.

3.6.1. What Does the Qur'an Represent for the Participants?

In the words of the participants, the Qur'an represents motivation to be better, something that allows them to continue and get up each day (in the mornings for prayer and recitation of the Qur'an). It is a refuge in difficult times, a challenge, a connection with Allah (swt), a guide for life, an instruction manual, a book from which they learn something new each time, a book through which Allah (swt) teaches something. It is like a friend whose company is enjoyed, and whose absence is felt when it is not studied or recited. It is a source of wisdom, blessings, positive energy, peace for the heart, and a cure for both material and immaterial afflictions. It is a guide and a guarantee of well-being for those who are conscious of God.

Their responses indicate two perspectives: one perspective sees the Qur'an as an active agent, and the other as a passive agent. The participants' perspective is that the Qur'an 'acts' in the sense that it has an effect on them by providing motivation, refuge, guidance, wisdom, blessings, positive energy, peace, curing afflictions, and teaching knowledge. On the other hand, they describe the Qur'an as a passive agent—an object, a book containing wisdom, an instruction manual, a friend waiting to be visited, a book waiting to be read and studied, a guarantee of good news for those who believe in God, and something that can help them connect with Allah (swt). The evidence suggests that the Qur'an is, at first, a passive agent and only acts or has an effect on the participants when the women who have converted to Islam make an effort to reach and access it, to listen, to read it, recite it, and study it, voluntarily taking on their role as learners and embarking on the learning journey.

From an andragogical perspective, 'teaching' is an activity carried out by the teacher and is different from 'learning' which is an activity carried out by the student (Knowles, 2001). I interpret this to mean that the Qur'an cannot teach, act, or have an effect unless the learner approaches and accesses it. The Qur'an transits from being a passive agent to an active one when the participants approach it with the desire to learn, understand it, and to access it. The effort comes first from the participants, from the female converts to Islam.

The evidence shows that at the time of conversion to Islam, the majority of the participants are not fully aware of 'what' or 'how' they need to learn to access the Qur'an in Arabic. At that moment, the Qur'an remains a passive agent until the woman becomes motivated and takes action to approach and access it, with the aim of finding and triggering the active agent and getting the benefits provided by the Sacred Book. This demonstrates that the participants are motivated as they seek ways and methods to access the Qur'an (see diagram 3.7).

The learner makes an effort to access the Qur'an in order to then receive its effects on themselves and their life.

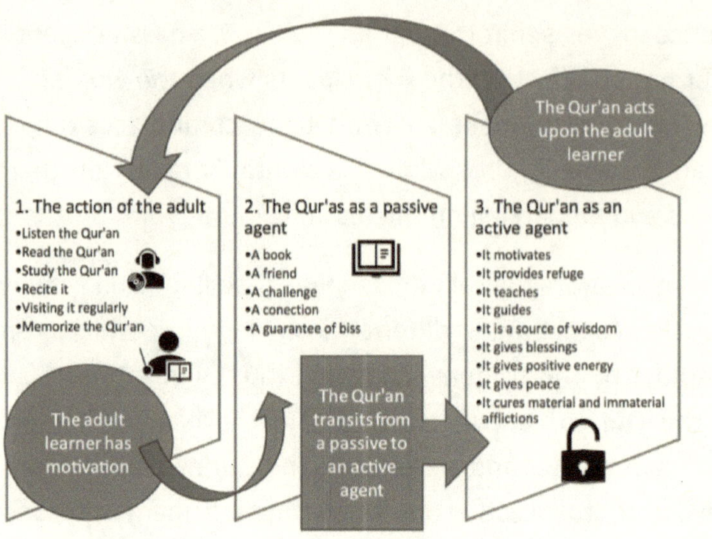

Figure 3.7. *The Qur'an as a Passive vs. Active agent according to the participants.*

3.6.2. Achievements and Positive Effects

The evidence suggests that the achievements and positive effects of accessing the Qur'an in its original language occur on three levels, each within different dimensions. At the interpersonal level in the educational dimension (meaning, interaction with peers or with teachers), at the personal level in the technical-practical and meaningful dimensions, and finally at the intrapersonal level in the cognitive, psychological, and spiritual dimensions (meaning, the inner self of the person). The order in which the evidence is presented does not imply that any one dimension is more important or significant for the participants than the others (see diagram 3.8).

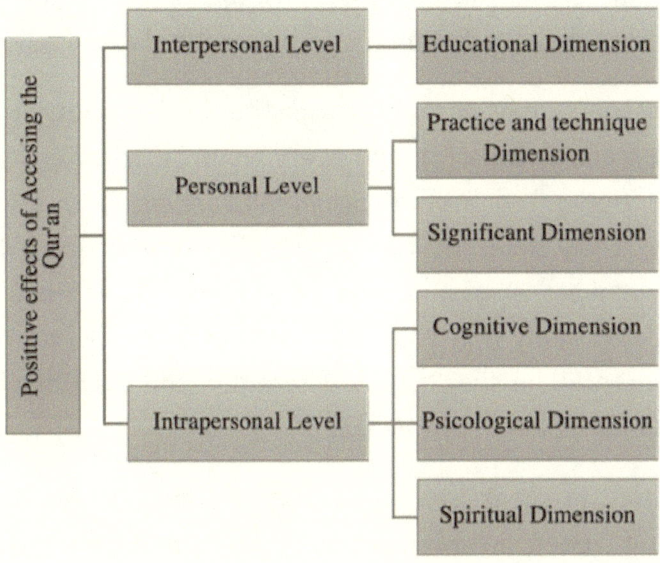

Figure 3.8. *Achievements and Positive Effects of Accessing the Qur'an.*

The female Muslim converts from Mexico and Colombia mentioned having achievements and positive effects on an interpersonal level, particularly in the educational dimension, by helping, teaching, motivating, or facilitating the studies of their own children. Their children, at various levels of depth, have studied, recited, and memorized the Qur'an. In the case of women who have had the opportunity to live and/or study abroad, their children have also learned Arabic. For the participants who have remained in their home countries, their children have had access to the Arabic alphabet, basic vocabulary, and conversation for greetings and introductions. However, living or studying abroad doesn't necessarily mean that they or their children maintain the same level of Arabic. Some of them mentioned losing understanding and communicative skills when they stop practicing, or they shared stories of other Latin

American women who converted to Islam and live in Arab countries but do not feel motivated to learn Arabic or access the Qur'an in Arabic. The following testimonies are presented as evidence:

> "My son studies at an Islamic institute (in a country that is not majority Muslim), and every week he tells me, 'Mom, I've memorized another *surah,*' and I feel happy, also I'm like, 'Okay, son, but it's not just about memorizing; think about what it says, analyze what it means, and see how you can apply it in your life.' And now, he talks to me so differently, he speaks very differently, and even helps me with my classes." (MC-3-MX)

> "I used to speak Egyptian Arabic very well, street Arabic, but it's been several years since I returned from Egypt to Colombia, and I just turned on a video here on YouTube, and I can see I've lost quite a lot, honestly, from not practicing." (KA-6-CL)

Another aspect of the educational dimension is the opportunity they have had to offer help, share, and teach other women within the community of Latin American Muslim converts (GC-5-MX, KA-6-CL, LH-7-CL, and LI-8-CL). One of them, of Mexican origin, has even taught and helped Arabic speakers memorize and correct *Tajweed*. This testimony breaks the taboo that only Arabic speakers have correct pronunciation. Here we see how a Mexican woman has developed *Tajweed* techniques to guide and teach people whose native language is Arabic (GC-5-MX).

The progress and achievements of their own children or other converts to Islam are also seen as achievements for them, as they dedicated time and effort to helping others to learn, which in turn motivates them to continue with their own studies. Additionally, all of them mentioned the opportunity to join study or reading groups focused on learning Arabic and/or *Tajweed*, whether informally or formally, in-person or online.

On a personal level and in the evolution of their own learning of Qur'anic recitation techniques, they mentioned achievements such as being able to recite the Qur'an fluently without stopping or getting stuck or making mistakes—some at a slower pace and others with greater fluency. Memorizing an entire *surah* or a complete *juzz* was also highlighted. Three of them mentioned having memorized the last part of the Qur'an, called *juzz amma*, completely, as well as other *suras* either in full or partially (GC-5-MX, LH-7-CL, and LI-8-CL), and one of them is close to finishing the memorization of *juzz amma* (SV-4-MX). Four of the participants mentioned that correcting incorrect memorization has been an important achievement (RM-1-MX, SU-2-MX, MC-3-MX, and SV-4-MX). One of them mentioned that achieving correct pronunciation while reciting is a major accomplishment (LI-8-CL), and another mentioned reciting half of *Surah Al-Baqarah* without errors and from memory, with *Tajweed* and *Tarteel*, in one hour and three minutes in front of several teachers as one of her most recent achievements (GC-5-MX). In general, all of them mentioned that developing the habit of reading and reciting the Qur'an is important.

Regarding the learning of the Arabic language, three of the participants mentioned the achievement of speaking, understanding, writing, and reading Egyptian Arabic and maintaining it (RM-1-MX, GC-5-MX, LI-8-CL). One of them reported completing all levels of classical Arabic in a formal institute (LH-7-CL), and another mentioned being enrolled in a formal online institute to study Qur'anic Arabic (LI-8-CL). In terms of the significant dimension, learning Arabic opens doors to understanding the Qur'an, its message, and the stories in it, and it is a very important achievement for them to recite and understand the Qur'an while reciting it without the need for translation (GC-5-MX, LH-7-CL, and LI-8-CL). Meanwhile, one of them reported that she requires two separate processes and moments: if she wants to recite, she focuses on the recitation and *Tajweed*, but if she wants to understand the meanings, she remains silent, reads silently while observing and consulting the meanings word-by-word using translations and dictionaries (SV-4-MX). Personally, this is the stage where I am as a student of the Qur'an. I have to give time and focus on recitation, and another time to read it and try to understand it word-by-word or with the help of translations and interpretations, whether in Spanish or English.

Three of the participants mentioned understanding the Qur'an through Arabic grammar (GC-5-MX and LI-8-CL), and one of them understands at least the grammar of the *suras* or *ayaat* she has already studied (KA-6-CL), which are part of the last section of the Qur'an. Five participants commented that studying *Tafseer* (interpretation) is an achievement in itself because they are reading about the context in which the *ayah* or *surah* was revealed, they are exploring Qur'anic vocabulary word-by-word and consulting at least one or two translations also known as interpretations (SV-4-MX, GC-5-MX, KA-6-CL, LH-7-CL, and LI-8-CL).

At the intrapersonal level, achievements and positive effects were observed in three dimensions: cognitive, psychological, and spiritual. Regarding the cognitive dimension, all the participants mentioned that having the opportunity to study the Qur'an, both its meanings and the recitation techniques, and understanding why it is important, brings them significant satisfaction. They also mentioned reflecting on the meanings of the Qur'an and being able to see the objectivity and practicality of the teachings and the wisdom of the message and the stories told in the Holy Book.

In the psychological dimension, they mentioned that studying the Qur'an is a source of motivation and commitment in itself. They also mentioned feeling a sense of belonging: "I belong to Allah (swt) and I belong to the group of people who submit to Allah (swt)" (SV-4-MX). All of them commented on feeling satisfaction from reading and/or understanding the words of Allah (swt), depending on each person's level of knowledge. Listening to the recitation or reciting the Qur'an reduces anxiety and despair (GC-5-MX), brings peace, tranquility, and a certain happiness (SU-2-MX), alleviates sorrow and sadness (LH-7-CL), helps them be patient and positive (SV-4-MX, GC-5-MX), and reminds them that they are human, with mistakes and temptations. When they don't engage in recitation, they feel something is missing, or they experience feelings of guilt, discomfort, and remorse for neglecting Allah's (swt) words, or sometimes due to negligence (SV-4-MX, GC-5-MX).

In the spiritual dimension, all participants mentioned experiencing benefits. Knowing that each letter recited is rewarded by Allah (swt), and even mistakes made are rewarded due to the intention of studying and approaching the Qur'an (RM-1-MX). They all commented that accessing the Qur'an elevates and strengthens their faith, and they feel connected to Allah (swt) or feel close to Him (swt). Here are some testimonies related to their connection with Allah (swt): "When reciting, reading, or studying the Qur'an, I feel that Allah (swt) is speaking to me personally and confirming the divine origin of the Qur'an" (LI-8-CL); "pronouncing the same words that Allah (swt) revealed to the Prophet (saw)" (SV-4-MX); "connecting with the unseen world—not only with Allah (swt) but also knowing that angels, *jinns*, and demons are there" (KA-6-CL); "the unseen world exists, and it's true, I don't see it as literature or fiction, but as the truth" (KA-6-CL); "sometimes the intellect doesn't understand, but the spirit connects with Allah (swt) through the Qur'an" (LH-7-CL).

They reported experiencing feelings of hope and refuge "when Allah (swt) says that He makes difficult things easier" (SV-4-MX, SU-2-MX, GC-5-MX), gratitude "for studying His Holy Book" (LI-8-CL), fear "when I am negligent" (SV-4-MX and GC-5-MX), or awareness of the existence and power of Allah (swt). They feel the need to dive deeper into studying the Qur'an to elevate their spirit (LH-7-CL, LI-8-CL), and they perceive the blessings of accessing the Qur'an: 'provision increases, and family sustenance lasts' (SV-4-MX), tranquility and peace 'from praying and practicing Allah's religion' (SU-2-MX, GC-5-MX), satisfaction 'from fulfilling Allah's Book' (GC-5-MX), and 'because I feel that accessing the Qur'an elevates us in rank with Allah (swt)' (SV-4-MX). See diagrams 3.9 and 3.10 for a better understanding of the achievements and positive effects of accessing the Qur'an in its original language.

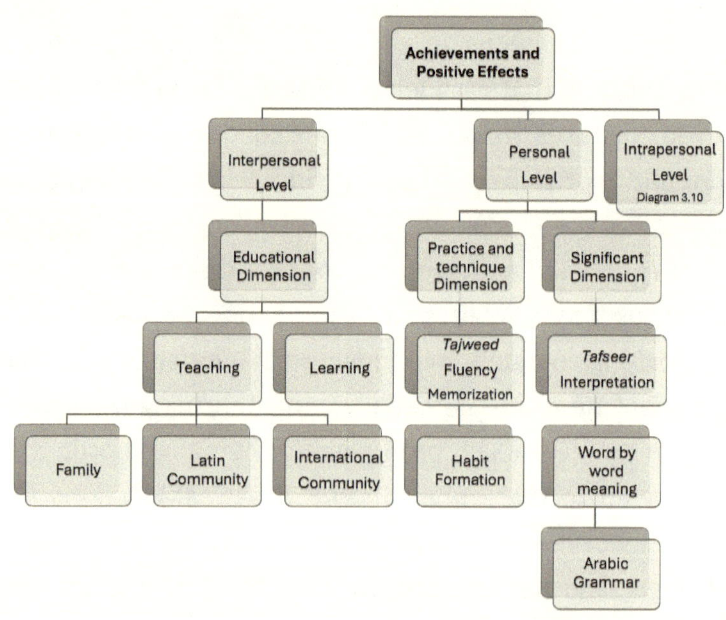

Figure 3.9. *Achievements and Positive Effects.* ***Interpersonal and Personal Levels***

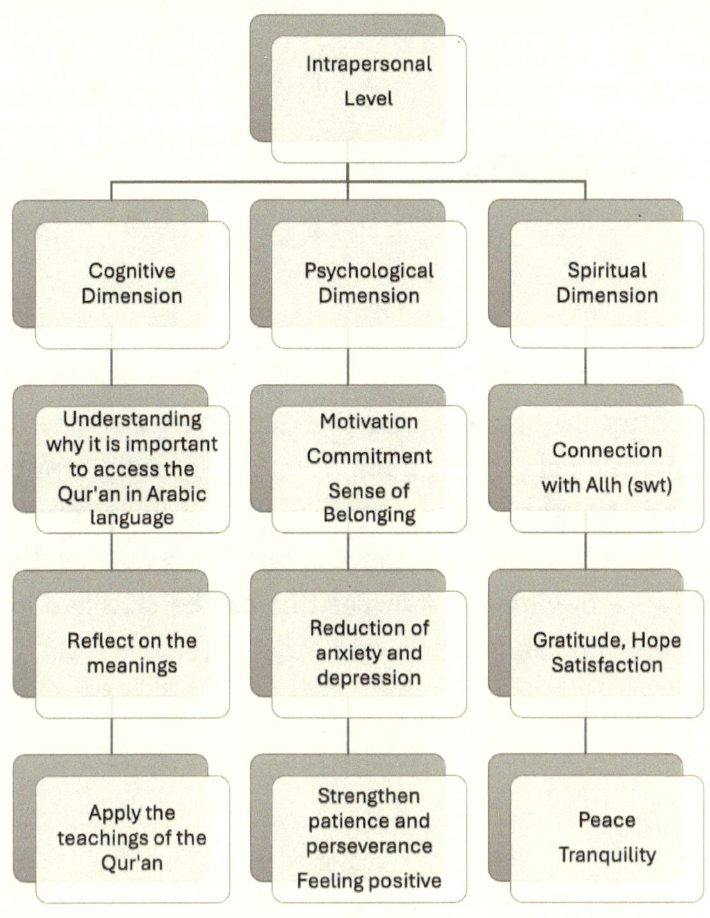

Figure 3.10. *Achievements and Positive Effects.* ***Intrapersonal Level***

Chapter 4

Conclusions

This study is about the learning journey of the Arabic language and recitation techniques to access the Qur'an in its original language among female converts to Islam from Mexico and Colombia. Their narratives highlight how the mind, heart, and body come together during the act of reciting the Qur'an. The evidence shows the performance of different activities that can be classified into three types: physiological, cognitive, and social. (See table 4.1).

Notes to the table 4.1

7 This is added according to the translations of the word "IQRA" from the Qur'an consulted on islamicity.org and Spanish translations by Melara Navío (1995), García (2013), and Cortés (2005).

8 Several participants mentioned it, but it is not developed in this study.

9 It is not addressed in this study, but it is one of the activities carried out through fatwas that are issued in Islamic communities, whether Muslim minority or majority.

Physiological activities involving the use of the body and the vocal apparatus	***Cognitive activities***	***Social activities***
Listening to the recitation. Repeating after someone recites. Reciting alone the Qur'an with *Tajweed rules*.	Reading and understanding a translation of the Qur'an. Reading the Qur'an in Arabic Studying Qur'anic Arabic and grammar. Studying and understanding the meanings of the Qur'an: Word-by-word (in Arabic) *Tafseer* (interpretation) Context of revelation Interpretation in the current context	Sharing and teaching what they are learning. Proclaiming[7] *Dawah*: religious proselytism[8] Jurisprudence: applying or requesting legislation presented in the Qur'an on a community, state, or national scale.[9]
Memorizing the Qur'an in Arabic, partially or completely, with or without understanding its meaning.		

Table 4.1. Activities to Access the Qur'an Among Female Muslim Converts from Mexico and Colombia

4.1. The Journey to Access the Qur'an

Each Muslim woman's journey is very unique, starting from different points and paths that gradually become clearer and align with a central trunk of knowledge. They enter this path to gain Qur'anic knowledge, starting with a translation of the Qur'an in their native language, sparking interest to start studying Arabic. Over time, they delve into *Tajweed* and *Tafseer*. They integrate information from previous experiences, their learning styles, their own topics of interest. They reflect upon the meanings of the Qur'an; different points of view and personal methods lead them through the journey. They expand step by step in knowledge, ascending in their personal, intellectual, emotional, psychological, and spiritual development (see diagrams 4.2 and 4.3).

The journey each women takes distinctly highlights the phases of deconstruction, construction, and strengthening of religious identity. They describe these phases as processes of building and deepening their faith. Accessing the Qur'an through a translation defines the moment of deconstruction, conversion to Islam and the pronouncement of the testimony of faith define the moment of construction, and the initiation and perseverance in studying the religion in general, Arabic, and Qur'anic recitation techniques in its original language define the moment of reinforcement of identity.

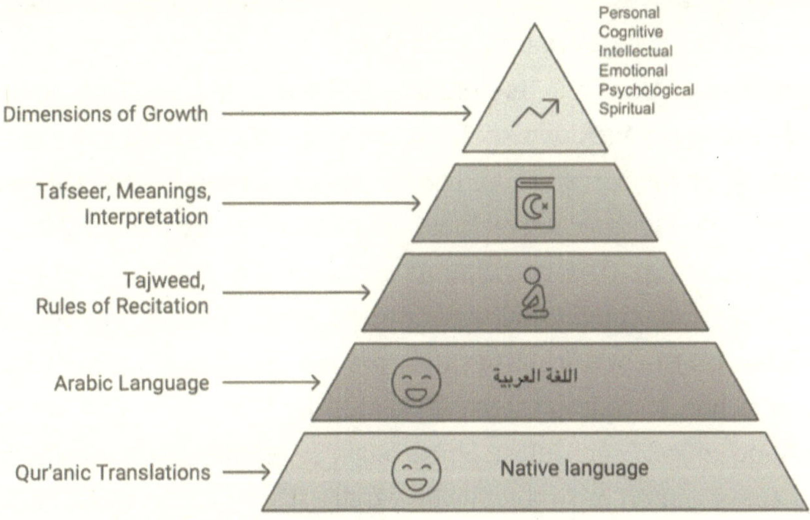

Figure 4.2. *Process of learning and growth among participants.*

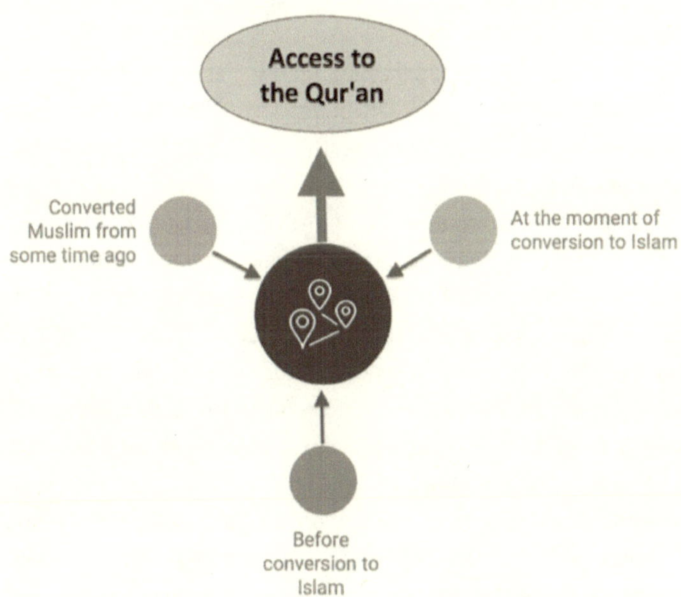

Figure 4.3. *Unique journey to access the Qur'an.*

The data was analyzed to map out each individual's journey and visualize the divergent points that lead to the common trunk of accessing the Qur'an in its original language. Based on the evidence obtained, it is concluded that, on the path to accessing the Qur'an in Arabic, participants see and are exposed to three paths: *Tajweed*, *Tafseer*, and Qur'anic Arabic[10], which includes vocabulary, grammar, and morphology. The participants choose to focus on one of these paths without completely ignoring the other two. Their decision depends on the opportunities they are exposed to, which vary from one another. A common starting point is the Arabic alphabet and the pronunciation of each letter. Some begin by learning basic vocabulary and conversation in Arabic, while others start directly with reading and recitation, usually using techniques for letter recognition, spelling, and then progressing to *Tajweed* rules to be able to read, repeat, and memorize the short *suras* of the Qur'an before moving on to the longer ones. The memorization of short *suras*, including

---

10 These were the topics addressed in this research, but Qur'anic studies also include: the names and attributes that Allah (swt) has granted to the Holy Book within the Qur'an, learning Qur'anic Arabic, Arabic grammar with application to the Qur'an, the rules and norms of recitation known as *Tajweed*, the interpretation of the Qur'an called *Tafseer*, the history of the Qur'anic revelation which goes hand in hand with the biography of the Prophet Muhammad (saw), and the reasons behind the names of each *surah*. Another topic related to Qur'anic studies is why and how the order of revelation differs from the sequential order in which we find the *suras* in the *Mushaf* (the term *Mushaf* is used to refer to the physical or printed book of the Holy Qur'an. In another language, we have Latinized the term and it is called "corans," although personally, I believe it would be more appropriate to use the plural "Books of the Qur'an"). Additionally, there is the etiquette for approaching the Qur'an, whether for reading, reciting, memorizing, or studying its meanings. This is one of the first topics that converts learn, as the purification ritual is the major ablution (*Ghusl*) and the minor ablution (*Wudu*), also used for prayers.

the opening *surah* of the Qur'an, serves to fulfill the second pillar of Islam, which is to pray five times a day.

The initial memorization process can be considered part of the construction of the religious identity of the converts, while engaging in reciting and memorizing more than *Surah Al Fatiha* can be considered as strengthening the religious identity as a Muslim. There is a branch of psychology that studies the relationship between memory and identity, often referred to as cognitive psychology, specifically within the areas of autobiographical memory and self-concept. Cognitive psychology examines how memory functions and influences our sense of self. The pioneer on cognitive psychology is Ulric Neisser (1967) who set the ground on the concepts and theories and research about memory and cognition (Neisser, 2014). There is a strong relationship between the creation of long-term memory and the construction of a person's identity (Conway & Pleydell-Pearce, 2000; McAdams, 2001; Souroujon, 2011).

The journey of conversion begins with each woman's initial steps—pronouncing the testimony of faith, wearing the Islamic scarf and modest clothing, navigating her first experiences as a Muslim within a non-Muslim society, forming connections with new Muslim peers either online or face-to-face, and striving to perform prayers accurately while making her first attempts at memorization. Each of these experiences leaves a lasting impression on the memory of the convert, gradually shaping her identity as a Muslim both inwardly and outwardly. McAdams (2001) explores how life narratives, formed and preserved in memory, contribute to personal identity. And Conway and Pleydell-Pearce (2000) discussed how the autobiographical memories form a basis for personal identity through the self-memory system. Once the convert is active in building her relationship with the Qur'an, looking for experiences through learning and understanding, making new relationships with people on the same path, creating memories of those experiences, and of course, willingly memorizing and wanting to understand the meanings of the Sacred Qur'an.

After their initial exposure to Qur'anic studies and their first memorization efforts, they consciously choose one of the study paths that is easiest for them. It is concluded that in adult learning within this context, Muslim converts persevere in the line of study where they experience more satisfaction and achievements to make objective and meaningful progress. This is a useful strategy to reduce frustration when it comes to learning Arabic, *Tajweed*, and engaging in Qur'anic studies in general, especially at the beginning of the learning journey. For example, some persevere in *Tajweed* and recitation rules, others focus on *Tafseer* (interpretation) and the context in which each *ayah* or *surah* was revealed, and others choose Qur'anic Arabic, seeking to understand the Qur'an through Arabic grammar and morphology. This is done without neglecting or abandoning the other two lines of study. A constant among the participants is that as they progress in their studies to access the Qur'an, they consciously choose their goals and objectives, and within their situational and contextual capacities, they seek study opportunities.

Another conclusion is that understanding the Qur'an, it is not necessary to learn Arabic for communication purposes; it is sufficient to read it, study, and memorize the meanings of the words, as well as to understand the grammar. In most cases, the participants access the meanings of the Qur'an through their native language, in this case, Spanish. When they focus solely on learning and practicing recitation, they use Spanish translations, and when they go into studying the meanings of the Qur'an, they achieve significant learning in Arabic and its grammar through different languages, such as English.

Regarding the technique of recitation, it is necessary to know and explore the vocal apparatus and all its components in what is called the anatomy of the voice to achieve melody, modulation, control of inhalation and exhalation, as well as strength and training of the vocal cords. Online courses increased during the Covid-19 lockdown, which demonstrated that technology and digitization facilitate their learning and help them achieve their study goals. It is important to seek correct and appropriate strategies for the digital environment, especially for teaching and learning *Tajweed*.

A single theoretical model is not enough to explain the phenomenon studied in this work. The learning process of Arabic and *Tajweed* among female converts to Islam in Mexico and Colombia is complex, as it involves the deconstruction, construction, and strengthening of religious identity, which impacts the women's daily lives, psychology, and emotions. To explain the phenomenon, a holistic theoretical framework is needed, focusing on investigating processes rather than products, understanding the nature of the process more than the results. The findings are explained through the andragogical model (Knowles, 2001), intrinsic motivation (Ryan & Deci, 2000), attention and concentration (Bruya & Tang, 2018; 2021), and finally, emotion regulation (Wadlinger & Isaacowitz, 2011).

4.2. Andragogy, Arabic and Tajweed

The experience of the female Muslim converts in learning Arabic and Qur'anic recitation can be understood as a journey of strengthening their religious identity. The andragogical model (Knowles, 2001) helps to understand the process and the elements involved. This model highlights the need for learners to be able to answer the 'what,' 'how,' and 'why' of learning something new. In general, the participants answered the question 'What to learn?'—accessing the Qur'an in its original language. They understand the 'why'—because it is the word of Allah (swt), the book revealed to the Prophet Muhammad (saw) in Arabic with a melodious recitation. As for the 'how,' they acknowledged that it took a long time to figure out. They described the process as 'hard, persistent, difficult, confusing, a challenge, and time-consuming,' only one participant described it as 'easy and smooth'. A common theme is that once they understood the process, the studies became familiar and accessible, and they felt capable of learning.

Regarding the learner's self-concept of the model (Knowles, 2001), the participants perceive themselves as adults with the ability to make decisions about their own lives. The evidence of this is their decision itself to convert to Islam and transform daily habits, as well as their perspectives and lifestyle. They gradually engaged in learning about the religion by their own choice. The evidence shows that the journey to study Arabic and Qur'anic recitation is different for each of them. The process of identity deconstruction can be observed when they enter a dynamic of self-recognition as adults with mental biases, habits, beliefs, and tendencies that they considered to change for something they consider better. This is a step that requires mental effort, willpower, and intrinsic self-observation.

In reference to their prior experience, their readiness to learn, and their inclination toward learning—which are the third, fourth, and fifth principles of the andragogical model (Knowles, 2001)—they draw upon their study skills, discipline, and reading habits to begin and persevere in their studies to access the Qur'an, as well as the material and immaterial resources they already possess. They also mentioned applying problem-centered learning, meaning they seek and find practical answers to situations that they consider challenging or problematic. They find intrinsic value in applying the teachings and wisdom of the Qur'an to practical matters and observe that it brings positive results within the sociocultural context they belong to. They feel satisfaction and personal reward in learning something new, as well as in achieving or reaching established goals.

The differences among the participants largely stem from whether they have the opportunity to study or live abroad versus staying in their places of origin. Marrying an Arab man, for example, facilitates daily interaction with the Arabic language and introduces an intercultural dynamic, requiring the challenge of adaptation to a new cultural environment. Conversely, marriage to someone from the same culture provides a unique opportunity to access the Qur'an together, allowing couples to learn side by side and apply Qur'anic teachings within their own cultural and native context. This approach, however, brings challenges, such as limited access to educational resources and teachers, unlike in a predominantly Arab or Muslim environment where such support is more readily available.

Economic resources are another difference among the converts, impacting—but not determining—their learning abilities. Some have financed their studies independently, either online or abroad, while others received financial aid or pursued free in-person and online courses. For most, the early stages of learning are informal, without structured goals or study plans—often a chance encounter on their path to conversion. However, one participant reported enrolling in an institute for foundational Islamic knowledge from the very beginning. The educational journey for Mexican and Colombian female Muslim converts generally progresses from informal to non-formal, which is the case of four participants of this study, the other four women enrolled to formal education in formal institutions for Arabic language and Qur'an. In informal education, there are no defined plans, goals, or objectives; in non-formal education, goals and objectives begin to take shape; and formal education includes structured plans, goals, objectives, and methodologies (Soto Kiewit et al., 2023).

All of the above are considered needs of the adult learner, which they address throughout their journey. This brings them happiness, satisfaction, and peace of mind, especially when they themselves define their actions and learning journey as 'something right' due to studying and accessing the Qur'an, the word of Allah (swt), which is for them the greatest source of motivation and where they find intellectual, emotional, psychological, and spiritual development.

Regarding social, community, and institutional growth (Knowles, 2001), they recognize that sharing what they are learning with more converts to Islam is important. Half of the participants mentioned offering classes and starting joint reading groups, which they consider their contribution to the Muslim community among the Latin American convert community. They also find an element of personal development in this, as the achievements of others represent achievements for themselves. From a spiritual perspective, they believe that sharing what they are learning brings rewards and elevates their spirit to be closer to Allah (swt).

The andragogical model (Knowles, 2001) considers that each learner has individual and situational differences, and that goals and purposes have different scopes, starting with individual growth, social growth, and community or institutional growth. The individual growth is something was described above with personal development in several dimension. As for social growth it can be seen when they share the knowledge they learn or when they apply the teachings of the Qur'an within in their relationships with others, in the way they take decisions and solve problems. However, the types of growth, such as social, community and the institutional need to be explored further in future research.

4.3. Driving Force Behind the Converts' Learning

Motivation to learn corresponds to the sixth principle of the andragogical model (Knowles, 2001). The type of motivation triggered in the participants is intrinsic motivation, which is sparked by active learning (Ryan & Deci, 2000). The participants' main motivation is the connection they achieve with Allah (swt) through accessing the Qur'an, and this is reinforced through active learning. It is concluded that their learning motivations evolve as they progress and achieve their learning goals and objectives. Progress and/or achievement of their goals represent a personal reward and a source of intrinsic motivation.

The andragogical model explains that in adult learning, feeling autonomous and making one's own decisions also reinforces intrinsic motivation because their learning goals and objectives are self-chosen, based on the 'I want to do it' rather than 'I have to do it' (Knowles, 2001; Ryan & Deci, 2000).

It was observed that the motivation to access the Qur'an among the participants is diminished by external circumstances, such as health problems, marriage, motherhood, travel, or other goals, such as religious proselytism, university or technical studies, or work-related matters. Motivation is also affected when Muslim women set ambitious, difficult-to-reach goals. They lose motivation and temporarily abandon their Qur'an studies and recitation. For example, when they achieve the goal of reciting and memorizing the last 10 or 15 *suras* of the Qur'an and their next goal is to recite and memorize *Surah Al-Baqarah*, the longest chapter, motivation tends to decline. In the words of one of them, women feel tired, overwhelmed, and uncomfortable (GC-5-MX).

4.4. The Mechanism to Achieve Learning

The mechanism to achieve both active learning and intrinsic motivation is to deploy attention and concentration. Attention involves directing the mind toward an activity and keeping it focused, while concentration is becoming absorbed in the activity and being distracted from everything else (Bruya & Tang, 2018; 2021). There are three types of attention: voluntary, involuntary, and fluid (Bruya & Tang, 2018). Based on the evidence provided in this study, it is concluded that the process of learning Arabic and Qur'anic recitation initially requires voluntary attention, as it demands significant cognitive and physical effort. The participants mention making considerable efforts to concentrate, especially when they are at the beginning of their journey, whether in Arabic or *Tajweed*.

After practicing and immersing themselves in learning, it becomes possible to deploy fluid attention, which has a specific goal but does not require significant effort and flows naturally (Bruya & Tang, 2021). This occurs when female converts to Islam achieve a goal and master the recitation technique (of a particular *surah* or *ayah*), and have gained a significant degree of knowledge in the Arabic language, whether in vocabulary, grammar, or morphology. It is important to mention that achieving a specific goal gives them self-confidence because they perceive that the effort decreases considerably, and they feel motivated when they see that fluid attention unfolds—meaning they can recite and understand that *surah* or *ayah* easily. It was also observed that achieving a specific goal does not necessarily imply the deployment of fluid attention for the reading and recitation of the entire Qur'an. The participants observed fluid attention for the *suras* or *ayaat* they practice or study constantly, if some new challenge or goal comes, then they repeat the process of giving full and voluntarily attention, keeping the practice and repetition and after a while they can deploy the fluid attention.

4.5. Emotion Regulation: An Essential Factor

The lack of emotional regulation affects or diminishes attention and concentration (Wadlinger & Isaacowitz, 2011), and it happens among the participants, the female Muslim converts from Colombia and Mexico, as they are emotionally impacted by the process of deconstructing and constructing their religious identity (Mondragón, 2023), which presents a challenge in their learning journey. The evidence shows that the participants enter a process of mental and emotional training where a cycle between attention and emotion regulation is observed. What enables them to activate this mental cycle is the constant repetition of a letter, a word, a phrase, an *ayah*, a *surah*, or fluid recitation with the fewest possible errors, depending on their level of learning and knowledge. This is why they mention finding 'refuge' in the recitation of the Qur'an because the rhythm of repetition and recitation helps them regulate their emotions, which in turn activates their attention and concentration, or vice versa—the attention they deploy while repeating or reciting allows them to regulate their emotions (see diagram 4.3). In the words of the participants, accessing and "reciting the Qur'an in Arabic is important because the intellect may not understand, but the spirit connects and does understand" (LH-7-CL). When emotions are very intense and difficult to regulate, they opt to listen and try to connect with the Qur'an through the recitation of professional reciters in order to regulate their emotions.

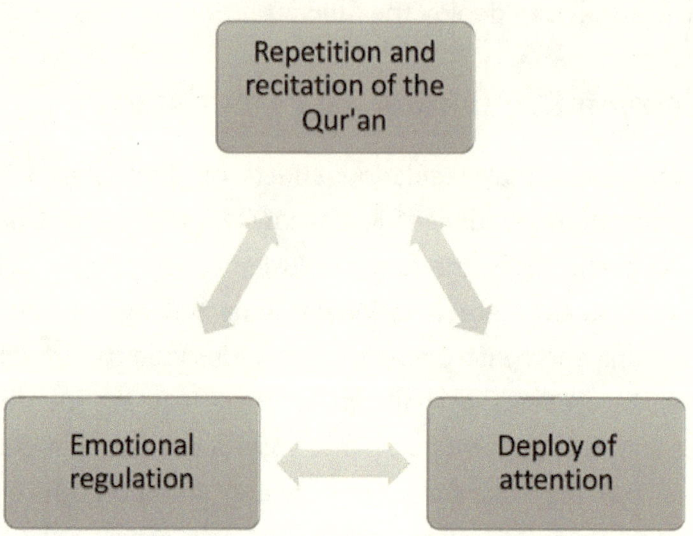

Figure 4.4. *Cycle between attention and emotion regulation as an effect of Qur'anic recitation.*

Chapter 5

Suggestions and Proposals

What suggestions or actions do these Muslim women propose to overcome the challenges and difficulties in the process of learning Arabic and Qur'anic recitation? The intention of collecting suggestions from the participants is to contribute to the creation and development of appropriate educational and didactic projects for Latin communities. The suggestions were classified into recommendations for: (1) other Latin women converts to Islam, (2) converts who are mothers of young children, (3) teachers, whether in-person or online, (4) the volunteers for learning support, (5) developers of digital learning applications, and (6) community leaders. The following paragraphs summarize the suggestions, most of which are in the words of the participants. My contribution as a researcher was in classifying, editing, and adding minimal suggestions based on my experience and observations.

Suggestions for Other Women Converts to Islam

When a person has just converted to Islam, it is important to make them feel like part of the community, part of Islam, and to foster integration. These individuals come with a strong desire to learn, and it is essential to take advantage of that by providing them with the information they ask for, without prejudice or taboos. This is the ideal time for them to learn how to pray, and those who already know how to pray should actively participate in teaching others. Prayer is a stepping stone to everything else.

It is never too late to start with the Qur'an, reading it, understand it, reciting it, whether someone has just converted or has been a Muslim for a long time. They should begin with translations in Spanish or their native language to understand the message. To do this, they should improve reading comprehension in their native language through short readings, because sometimes our societies do not use to read often. Learning how to pray starts with transliterations and audio, but they should also learn the Arabic letters at the same time. Once they have learned the Arabic alphabet, transliteration should be avoided or used only occasionally because it makes a significant impact on the pronunciation and the meaning of what is being said.

It is important to start, create, or maintain a relationship with the Qur'an. Everyone is in a different situation, and at the very least, reading the translation is fine, as that is within their capability. At the very least, it should be in sight on your table or desk or on a suitable place where the person can see it only by passing by, and eventually, the person should open it. Even if they don't know how to read it in Arabic language, just seeing the letters and their shapes can help. If they have a *Mushaf* (the book of the Qur'an in Arabic) with *Tajweed* rules in color, it is visually attractive, and the heart becomes drawn to it just by looking. Everyone finds their own path to Allah (swt), any small steps count.

Consistency makes you an expert. Dedicate 20 to 30 minutes every day to review and repeat. YouTube videos and audio recordings help; repeat after the audio and listen to them during your daily activities, including household chores, or while driving to work or school. Be patient, be disciplined, ask Allah (swt) to make it easier for you, and don't give up. To understand the meanings of the Qur'an, I advise using translations, finding websites that break down the meaning of each word, and referring to *Tafseer*. Don't worry if you get stuck, if your tongue stumbles, or if your memory fails—it's normal, and it happens to all of us. Eliminate the 'I can't' thoughts through practice and repetition.

Repeat the word or phrase several times, starting slowly until the muscles in your mouth adjust, and gradually achieve fluency. Understand that teachers have to correct the students, and sometimes these corrections can feel overwhelming because the sounds don't come out correctly from our tongue, lips, or throat. Both students and teachers need to have humility and know the proper etiquette for learning and approaching Allah's (swt) Holy Book. It's important to have good manners in giving and receiving corrections, to make your best effort, and if it becomes tiring, rest and try again the next day. Each day of practice and study brings a little more progress. When enrolling in courses, be present in class and avoid trying to read other chats at the same time. The Qur'an requires full attention, focus on paying of your attention and practicing vocal exercises often.

Arabic language and Qur'anic reading go hand in hand, and they must be studied simultaneously, with Arabic grammar gradually introduced. A person entering Qur'anic studies must understand that it's a lifelong commitment, and it can't be any other way. It's important to set goals with the Qur'an—achievable objectives and not overwhelm—and try to achieve those objectives before setting new ones. But also avoid setting tests or goals against the clock; it is very stressful.

The motivation to be a self-learner is vital. The adult learner must sit down to study and practice without being told to do so, organizing their activities and time and finding their own way. All participants mentioned repeating aloud as the main technique, while others write the words in Arabic multiple times. Understanding what is being recited or learned through translations is also key. Identify a *surah* or *ayah* that has special meaning to the student, start with that phrase, write it in a notebook, read the story of when it was revealed, see what each word means, and thus develop a connection with that *surah* or *ayah*. What is memorized should be integrated into the *salat*, the prayer.

Remember the importance of intention and sincerity when approaching the Qur'an. Allah (swt) blesses us with understanding, correct pronunciation, and His blessings, so sincerity means doing it for Allah (swt). Understand that sometimes the results may not be what we expect or desire because the effort is made by the student, but the results belong to Allah (swt). However, do not let that discourage you because every attempt, every practice counts and is rewarded.

Suggestions for Muslim women converts who are mothers of young children.

Sometimes the convert mothers feel hesitant to teach their children the Qur'an, the prayers, the Islamic principles. It is important that mothers talk to their children about Allah (swt), about values and religion, and teach them how to pray, how to make supplications. Sometimes studying with them can be a source of motivation for the mothers to study as well. Children are imitators, we as mothers must include them in religious activities, studies, and recitation by example, by doing ourselves as mothers, without imposing on them, but they must be invited, and they will naturally follow what their mother does. Provide them with age-appropriate activities that focus on Islam and the Qur'an. And if the mother wants to learn and attend online classes, and they have young children, they can organize themselves, settle the time and space. It is possible to have them in their arms or very close by, with their toys, food, water, and everything they need for the two or three hours of the class.

Suggestions for study techniques. It is important to have a 'preferred' space, which is comfortable, well-lit, and quiet. Organize study materials, whether physical, such as the study *Mushaf*, pencils, colors, a notebook, and digital materials. Have organized folders with files for exercises to print or consult, digital books on *Tajweed* rules, and save links to frequently used websites, such as Arabic dictionaries, translators, word-by-word meanings, *Tafseer*, and translations. Subscribe to YouTube channels that offer repetitions of *ayaat* or *suras*, pronunciation exercises for each letter, or lectures discussing the *Tafseer* of a particular *surah* and its importance.

Suggestions for reciting every day. It is an Islamic tradition to dedicate time before or after the *Fajr* prayer to reciting the Qur'an (*Fajr* means at morning prayer). My suggestion is to do it whenever there is available time, at any hour of the day or night. Sometimes it works to dedicate 10 minutes during each prayer exclusively to practicing recitation, sometimes it works to do it before going to sleep, and sometimes it works on the go from one place to another. The important thing is to access the Qur'an every day, even if it's just one *ayah*, because that is your capacity. After a week or two of practicing that *ayah*, you move on to the next, and soon you will have two *ayaat*, then three, and so on.

It is important to have a manageable amount of recitation each day according to your level (it could be three *ayaat*, one or two full pages, a complete medium-length *surah*, or a full *juz*), and always try to understand what you are reading or reciting in Arabic. Take time to reflect. Understand the seriousness of abandoning the Qur'an. It's like going on a hunger strike, leaving the spirit without nourishment.

When there is mental exhaustion, for example at in-person or online classes, take a break, refresh yourself, take a bath, or go for a walk. When the exhaustion is extreme or there is a lot of stress, listen to recitation and relax. Reflect on the part that is being studied or recited, and consider how it can be applied to everyday life or the context in which you live. You can write down these reflections on a diary.

Suggestions for Teachers:

An online or in-person teacher must constantly renew their intention to teach and remember that they are teaching for the sake of Allah (swt). They need to work on their own faith and motivation. Teaching can also be very frustrating because classes for women are often intermittent due to health, marriage, and motherhood. Courses get cancelled due to a lack of students, and it becomes necessary to reconvene. This is why sincerity is very important in teaching—it is done for Allah (swt) to gain His pleasure and reward, and not to focus too much on the results, as that is an area that belongs to Allah (swt). It is possible to be systematic and measure results, but the motivation to teach should not diminish because of them.

The teacher should ensure that the student understands why it is important to access the Qur'an in Arabic, why it is essential to learn *Tajweed*, and the meanings of the words in Arabic. This should be done out of love for Allah (swt), as it is the strongest source of motivation, driven by the desire to draw closer and connect with Him (swt) through His Holy Book. However, to understand this, it is important to teach the 'six pillars of faith' before the 'five pillars of Islam' because the pillars of faith are the foundation of the pillars of Islam, which are essentially religious practices that, without faith, do not mean much to a convert.

The participants' opinions on having gender-segregated in-person classes are divergent, especially given the context of Muslims in Latin America, where they are a minority. In general, they commented that this would be ideal but is not always possible. Some participants feel the need to have female teachers to teach exclusively to women, and the same for male students with male teachers. The suggestion is that when local mosques and *musallas* organize an Arabic and *Tajweed* course, the classroom should be divided so that men sit on one side and women on the other. This is done in Malaysia, for example, and the students do not face each other, but all look toward the board or the front.

In-person teachers should use more active techniques to encourage greater student participation. It is important to understand that the Latin American context is different from that of Arab or Asian Muslim-majority countries. Teachers must observe the community and find an appropriate method of teaching; however, the participants did not specify exactly how. One of them mentioned returning to the teaching method of the Prophet Muhammad (saw), but did not elaborate on it. A suggestion from the literature review is to implement 'voice warm-up' activities for 10 to 15 minutes at the start of the class, also called pronunciation exercises (Supriyadi & Julia, 2019), with students standing and reciting the complete alphabet in unison along with the vowel movements. This is applicable for in-person classes.

The suggestions for both online and in-person teachers are to keep groups small—no more than 10 people, possibly five—to give students the time and attention they need, so they don't have to wait too long for their turn to recite. The participants need support, as it's easy for them to feel discouraged, incapable, or that they are not progressing. Pairing up students could be a solution. If there are six students in the class, assign pairs so they can follow up on each other, or if they are spouses, they can motivate each other, agree on practice times outside of class, and check in when one is absent. With the pairing technique, students receive support and continuity in their studies.

Assistants or helpers play an important role in teaching. They assist with recitation, repetitions, and corrections, organize the participants' turns, and track progress, not only through attendance records but also by noting what has been recited and identifying the errors that need to be corrected. If the class is online, the assistant can continue with the class if the teacher leaves or gets disconnected, or if the teacher is unable to attend one day.

Teachers must have humility and their own ethical behavior when teaching, according to what is culturally accepted as good ethics and behavior during a class. Explaining how the class will be conducted is very helpful, as well as explaining the benefits, also informing about the difficulties that others have encountered, and making it clear that the class is about repeating, correcting, and repeating again. Allow students the freedom to leave the class when they are mentally exhausted without being offended. Teachers should understand that they, too, make mistakes, and sometimes the student will notice. It's important to be humble and accept the error, making it easier to continue with the class. They should have patience, as not everyone learns at the same pace, and they should avoid rushing the students because under stress, the brain starts to block, especially for beginners.

Online classes are different from in-person formats. In sessions where the teacher says the *ayah* and everyone repeats it at the same time, this method doesn't work online. Instead, the teacher should go one by one, with each student taking turns to recite an *ayah*, ensuring to mute the microphones during other students' recitations. Online teachers must learn how to use digital tools and understand what can be done, as online classes are the most accessible option for many Muslims in the diaspora. For a Muslim convert in diaspora or geographically isolated, with the intention to learn Arabic and Qur'anic recitation, the first step may be to build foundational skills in technological literacy.

Teachers must be aware of the characteristics and culture of the Muslim convert population in Mexico and Colombia, and arguably across Latin America. It's a challenge due to heterogeneous community. These are adults capable of making their own life decisions, choosing what they learn, absorb, or set aside. However, they also carry personal biases and established ways of doing things to achieve their goals. As fully independent adults, they may sometimes find it challenging to accept corrective feedback on their mistakes. It is not possible to teach an adult the same way you would teach a child. Adults tend to feel offended when corrected. It's important to consider the prior experiences of adult learners, as well as to explain the content of the classes, the format, the ethical behavior expected, and the opportunity to ask questions and actively participate in their own learning, especially when there is confusion, stress, or frustration. Encourage them to talk about the problems they observe and invite them to propose solutions. The teacher becomes a facilitator, adviser, and companion in the learning process for converts to Islam. It's essential to understand that each student is in a different situation, and sometimes they are not ready to receive or learn technical information like *Tajweed* or Arabic language. However, they can access the Qur'an through translations, *Tafseer* classes and interpretation, joint readings in their native language, and community reflection and support groups during the process of converting to Islam in a Latin American context. Inform them of the importance of accessing the Qur'an in its original language, and invite them to take classes when they feel ready to do so.

Suggestions for Volunteers

Helpers and volunteers will always be needed, and if they have an ability to learn or advance a little further in Arabic or recitation, they must understand that it is a gift and a blessing from Allah (swt) and that they should not feel superior to the other students. They need to work on their ego because they may feel superior to others. They should have an attitude of helping and serving, which truly requires humility. Helpers and volunteers need to examine their intentions—whether they are doing it for Allah (swt) or to stand out and feel better than others. Volunteers and helpers must commit to their own studies and to the group of students they are assisting.

Suggestions for Community Leaders, Sheikhs and Imams.

They must commit to their own studies and recitation because sometimes it is very obvious that they do not know how to pronounce (for example) the opening supplications of the *Khutbah* (Friday sermon) correctly, or those leading the *salat* (prayer) need to take the responsibility of memorizing more of the Qur'an and doing so correctly. The Arab sheikhs and Imams coming to Mexico and Colombia from abroad need to do efforts to understand the Latin American culture. Arabic and *Tajweed* classes are important, and there is a need for spaces where people can connect with the Qur'an. Alongside that, awareness campaigns are needed to raise consciousness and motivate the community by explaining the benefits and rewards of making the effort to read, recite, and study the Qur'an in its original language. For example, this can begin in the

Khutbahs or Friday sermons, where the importance of accessing the Qur'an in Arabic is promoted.

Creating and promoting a short- and medium-term plan or projection for the self-study. It would be beneficial to have community goals for the classes, such as participating in local competitions at our level focused on Qur'an memorization or fluent readings. Starting with *Al-Fatiha*, half of a *juz'*, or *juz' Amma*, which is the last part of the Qur'an. This would be an important motivational factor. It could be organized by country and then on a Latin American level.

Suggestions for Developers of Digital Applications and Websites.

Existing applications should be expanded and translated into Latin American Spanish, if possible, as many are available only in English. Courses and tutorials on how to use these applications should be offered, as many converts are not familiar with technology and digitalization.

Opportunities for Future Research

A review was conducted on second-language acquisition theories (Gardner, 1976; Haron et al., 2016; Krashen, 1981; Krashen & Terrell, 1983; Moghazy, 2021; Omar, 2017), which generally focus on social communication for external rewards such as marriage, employment, migration, or studies. These theories were excluded in this work because the purpose is to observe the learning process to access the Qur'an. However, second-language learning theories represent an opportunity for studying the construction and strengthening of religious identity among Latin American converts, mostly for the converts living abroad.

The construction of Muslim identity studied from the perspective of cognitive psychology is a good topic for future research. What is the relationship between narratives of the converts and identity formation? and what is the relationship between memorization of the Qur'an and identity? These questions represent an opportunity to explore in the context of Latin American Muslims converts.

Online programs and digital applications are ways to learn the religion among converts in Latin America and it is important to explore this aspect in future research, what are the impacts they have? what are the best strategies to implement? how the applications can be developed to have better results on the Latin American Muslim converts? (Wahid et al., 2019; Alagrami & Eljazzar, 2020; Muhammad et al., 2012).

The andragogical model views adult education as fostering individual, social, community, and institutional growth (Knowles, 2001). This research primarily focused on individual development and touched some social impacts of learning activities among these women. However, aspects like social, community, and institutional growth warrant further exploration in future studies. What impacts can -studying the Arabic language and Qur'an recitation- have on social, community, and institutional levels?

This study included only female Muslim converts. It would be interesting to gather the experiences of male converts to Islam and their process of learning the Arabic language and Qur'anic recitation techniques. I am also very curious to delve deeper into the topic of interculturality and how daily interactions with other Muslim cultures impact the construction of identity among Latin female converts.

References

Aboelezz, M. (2015). A History of the Arabic Language and the origin of non-dominant varieties of Arabic. In C. M. Rudolf Muhr, Kelen Ernesta Fonyuy, Zeinab Ibrahim (Ed.), *Pluricentric Languages and non-dominant Varieties worldwide: Pluricentric Languages across continents - Features and usage.* (pp. 11–24).

Abualkishik, A. & Omar, K. (2008). Quranic Braille System. *International Journal of Computer, Electrical, Automation, Control and Information Engineering, 2*(10), 3306–3312. http://www.waset.org/publications/7971

Al Isharah (2022). *The BSL Qur'an Project.* https://www.alisharah.com/services/the-bsl-quran-project/

Alagrami, A., & Eljazzar, M. (2020). SMARTAJWEED: Automatic Recognition of Arabic Quranic Recitation Rules. *Computer Science & Information Technology (CS & IT)*, 145–152. https://doi.org/10.5121/csit.2020.101812

Alkhateeb, Firas. (2014). *Lost Islamic history: reclaiming Muslim civilisation from the past.* C. Hurst & Co. (Publishers) Ltd.

Allah, S. N. D. K., Mokhtar, W. K. A.W., Jaafar, S. S., Ibrahim, A., Khairuldin, W. M. K. F.W., Imas, M. M., Razali, M. A. T. M., Amiruddin, E., & Jamaludin, A. S. (2020). The Lacking of the

Quran's Recitation within Society: An Initial Review. *International Journal of Academic Research in Business and Social Sciences, 10*(12), 69–77. https://doi.org/10.6007/ijarbss/v10-i12/8217

Al-Qwidi, M. (2002). Understanding the Stages of Conversion to Islam, the Voices of British Converts [Doctoral Thesis]. In *University of Leeds*. https://www.researchgate.net/publication/41201524_Understanding_the_Stages_of_Conversion_to_Islam_The_Voices_of_British_Converts (Accessed on December 2020).

Ancos, V. de. (2009). Anatomía y fisiología de la voz humana. In *Lo uno y lo múltiple: Homenaje a Félix del Valle y Díaz* (pp. 703–731). https://realacademiatoledo.es

Ariffin, S., Abdullah, M., Suliaman, I., Ahmad, K., Deraman, F., Shah, F. A., Mohd Yusoff, M. Y. Z., Abd Razzak, M. M., Mohd Noor, M. M., Meftah, J. T., Kasar, A. K., Amir, S., & Mohd Nor, M. R. (2013). Effective techniques of memorising the Quran: A study at Madrasah tahfiz Al-quran, Terengganu, Malaysia. *Middle East Journal of Scientific Research, 13*(1), 45–48. https://doi.org/10.5829/idosi.mejsr.2013.13.1.1762

Asad, M. (1980). *The Message of The Qur'an*. https://islamicbulletin.org/en/ebooks/quran/quran_asad.pdf

(Accessed on July 2023)

Auwal, S. M., Abubakar, H.H., & Yusuf, I. (2018). *The Effect of Quranic Recitation and Listening to It on the Believers' Hearts*. Retrieved from http://www.academia.edu

Berg, B. L. (2001). *Qualitative Research Methods for the Social Sciences* (K. Hanson, Ed.; 4th ed.). A Pearson Education Company.

Bishop, B. (1998). *A History of the Arabic Language*. Brigham Young University. https://doi.org/10.2307/1595864

https://linguistics.byu.edu/classes/Ling450ch/reports/arabic.html

(Accessed on July, 2023)

Bruya, B., & Tang, Y. (2018). Is Attention Really Effort? Revisiting Daniel Kahneman's Influential 1973 Book Attention and Effort. *Frontiers in Psychology. 9*(September), 1–10. https://doi.org/10.3389/fpsyg.2018.01133

Bruya, B., & Tang, Y. (2021). Fluid Attention in Education: Conceptual and Neurobiological Framework. *Frontiers in Psychology, 12*(September). https://doi.org/10.3389/fpsyg.2021.704443

Cañas Cuevas, S. (2015). The Politics of Conversion to Islam in Southern Mexico. In A. Khan (Ed.), *Islam and the Americas* (pp. 163–185). University Press of Florida.

Che Noh, M. A., Kasan, H., Yusak, Y. M., & Yusuf, S. A. M. (2019). Strategic Management of Qur'anic Recitation Teaching Among Primary School Teachers in Malaysia. *AL-HAYAT: Journal of Islamic Education, 3*(1), 1–8. https://doi.org/10.35723/ajie.v3i1.39

Che Noh, M. A., Tamuri, A. H., Razak, K. A., & Suhid, A. (2014). The Study of Quranic Teaching and Learning: United Kingdom Experience. *Mediterranean Journal of Social Sciences, 5*(16), 313–317. https://doi.org/10.5901/mjss.2014.v5n16p313

Colón, J. V. (2014). *Una ciencia noble... Introducción al tayuíd*. Guayabera Media. Google Books.

Conway, M. A., & Pleydell-Pearce, C. W. (2000). The Construction of Autobiographical Memories in the Self-Memory System. *Psychological Review, 107*(2), 261–288. https://doi.org/10.1037/0033-295X.107.2.261

Cook, A. B. S., & Yucel, S. (2022). Soundness of the Heart: An Analysis of the Unique Qualities of the Qalb Salim. *Teosofi: Journal Tasawuf Dan Pemikiran Islam, 12*(1), 1–21. https://doi.org/10.15642/teosofi.2022.12.1.1-21

Cook, D. A., & Artino, A. R. (2016). Motivation to learn: an overview of contemporary theories. *Medical Education, 50*(10), 997–1014. https://doi.org/10.1111/medu.13074

Corriente, F. (2002). Acerca de la transcripción o transliteración del código grafémico árabe al latino, particularmente en su variante castellana. *Miscelánea de Estudios Árabes y Hebraicos, Sección Árabe-Islam, 51*, 361–368.

Cortés, J. (2005). *El Sagrado Corán. Versión castellana*. Centro Cultural Islámico Fátima Az-Zahra.

Czerepinski, K. C. (2000). *Tajweed Rules of the Quran, Part One*. Retrieved from https://www.muslim-library.com/dl/books/english_Tajweed_Rules_of_the_Quran.pdf (Accessed on November, 2023).

DGDH Facultad de Psicología. (2022, May 9). Trabajemos en la Tolerancia a la Frustración. *Gaceta de La UNAM*, 14–16. https://www.gaceta.unam.mx/trabajemos-en-la-tolerancia-a-la-frustracion/ (Accessed on July, 2023).

Embarek, M. (2000). ¿Para quién se escribe?, ¿para quién se traduce? El caso de la literatura marroquí. In *Orientalismo, exotismo y traducción* (pp. 237–242). Universidad de la Universidad de

Castilla-La Mancha. Retrieved from https://bit.ly/3BpVsfA (Accessed on November 2, 2023).

Epalza, M. de. (2003). El Corán y sus Traducciones: Algunos Problemas Islamológicos y de Traducción, con Propuestas de Soluciones. In *El Islam Plural* (pp. 379–400). Icaria Editorial.

Fernández-Alcántara, M., García-Caro, P. M., Pérez-Marfil, N. M., & Cruz-Quintana, F. (2013). Experiencias y obstáculos de los psicólogos en el acompañamiento de los procesos de fin de vida. *Anales de Psicología, 29*(1), 1–8. https://doi.org/10.6018/analesps.29.1.139121

Flick, U. (2009). *An introduction to qualitative research*. Sage Publications, Inc.

Fort, X. (2017). *Cómo funciona la voz: la producción de sonido*. Retrieved from https://www.xescafort.com (Accessed July 20, 2022).

García, I. (2013). *Traducción Comentada. El Corán*. https://doi.org/10.2307/602217

García, R. J. (2014). *Las Mujeres Conversas del Centro Educativo de la Comunidad Musulmana en la Ciudad de Mexico. Construcción de una Identidad Religiosa.* (Thesis for Master Degree) Universidad Nacional Autónoma de Mexico.

Gardner, R. C. (1976). Second Language Acquisition: A Social Psychological Perspective. *The Oxford Handbook of Applied Linguistics, (2 Ed.)*. https://doi.org/10.1093/oxfordhb/9780195384253.013.0014

Ghadim, N. A., Jomhari, N., Alias, N., Mohd Rashid, S. M., & Mohd Yusoff, M. Y. Z. (2013). Mother's Perspective Toward al-Quran

Education for Hearing Impaired Children in Malaysia. *Malaysian Online Journal of Educational Technology, 1*(4), 26–30. www.mojet.net

Haque, A. (2017). Concept of the Heart in Islam. *Islamic Psychology Meeting for Study and Research in New Delhi, India.*

Haron, S. C., Hassanien, I., Mamat, A. A., Rusli, W., Fouad, W. A., & Rawash, M. M. (2016). Challenges in Learning to Speak Arabic. *Journal of Education and Practice, 7*(24), 80–85. https://www.iiste.org/Journals/index.php/JEP/article/view/32603

Hassan, S. S. Bin & Zailaini, M. A. Bin. (2013). Analysis of Tajweed Errors in Quranic Recitation. *Procedia - Social and Behavioral Sciences, 103*, 136–145. https://doi.org/10.1016/j.sbspro.2013.10.318

Hosein, I. (2020). *The Quran and the Moon.* Imran N. Hosein Publications. Retrieved from http://www.imranhosein.org (Accessed on November, 2022).

HADI (Human Assistance and Development International, 2024). Web page: *IslamiCity.org*. https://doi.org/EIN: 95-4348674. (Accessed December, 2020).

Khan, N., Ahmad, N. B., Abdalla, A. N., & Nubli, M. (2010). Mental and spiritual relaxation by recitation of the holy Quran. *2nd International Conference on Computer Research and Development, May*, 863–867. https://doi.org/10.1109/ICCRD.2010.62

Knowles, M. (2001). *Andragogía. El aprendizaje de los adultos.* AlfaOmega Grupo Editor.

Krashen, S. D. (1981). Second language acquisition and Second Language Learning. In *The Routledge Handbook of Applied*

Linguistics (First Inte). Pergamon Press Inc. https://www.sdkrashen.com/content/books/sl_acquisition_and_learning.pdf

Krashen, S. D., & Terrell, T. D. (1983). *The Natural Approach: Language Acquisition in the Classroom*. Prentice Hall Europe.

Leavy, P. (2017). *Research Design: Quantitative, Qualitative, Mixed Methods, Arts-Based, and Community-Based Participatory Research Approaches*. Guilford Publications, Inc.

Macdonald, M. C. A. (2008). The Evidence for Old Arabic. In K. Versteegh, M. Eid, A. Elgibali, M. Woidich, & A. Zaborski (Eds.), *Encyclopedia of Arabic Language and Linguistics: Vol. III* (pp. 464–477). Brill.

Mansson, M. A. (2006). *Becoming Muslim: Western Women's Conversions to Islam*. Palgrave Macmillan.

McAdams, D. P. (2001). The psychology of life stories. *Review of General Psychology, 5*(2), 100–122. https://doi.org/10.1037/1089-2680.5.2.100

Medina, A. (2012). *Islam e Identidad Musulmana en Guadalajara en Proceso de Relocalización* (Master Thesis). El Colegio de Jalisco A.C.

Medina, A. (2017). Pensar el Islam en tiempo de movilidad: para una etnografía en América Latina. *Ruta Antropológica, 6*, 36–69.

Medina, A. (2018). El Islam en Mexico. Revisión Histórica de su Inserción al Escenario Religioso Mexicano. *Vuelo Libre. Revista de Historia, 5*, 1–17.

Medina, A. (2019). *Islam-latino. Identidades étnico-religiosas. Un Estudio de Caso Sobre los Mexicanos Musulmanes en Estados Unidos* (First). El Colegio de Jalisco A.C.

Medina, A. (2023). "Dios enseña cómo pedir". Una musulmana en Guadalajara. In *De la religiosidad vivida a la religiosidad bisagra* (Primera Ed, pp. 601–622). Casa Chata.

Melara Navío, A. G. (1996). *El Noble Corán y su traducción-comentario en Lengua Española*. Complejo del Rey Fahd.

Moghazy, M. (2021). Teaching and Learning Arabic as a Second Language: A Case Study of Dubai. *International Journal of Science and Engineering Applications, 10*(05), 052–061. https://doi.org/10.7753/ijsea1005.1002

Mohamad, S. P., Yusoff, M. Y. Z., & Hasan Adli, D. S. (2013). Sound Therapy through Quranic Recitation in Dealing with Emotional and Verbal Motor Skills Problems of Children with Autism. *QURANICA, International Journal of Quranic Research*, *5*(2), 53–72.

Mohd Daud, N. A., Jomhari, N., & Abdull Zubi, N. I. (2012). FAKIH: A Method to Teach Deaf People "Reading" Quran. *The 2nd Annual International Qur'anic Conference 2012*, 53–67.

Mondragón, G. (2023). *En Búsqueda de la Religión: Cómo las Mujeres Musulmanas están Encontrando el Islam*. Editorial Maktaba. Colombia.

Mossad, A. E. (2017). *The Challenges of Translating the Quran*. Globalization Partners International. https://www.globalizationpartners.com/2017/07/13/the-challenges-of-translating-the-quran/ (Accessed on July 4, 2022)

Mottaghi, M. E., Esmaili, R., & Rohani, Z. (2011). Effect of Quran recitation on the level of anxiety in athletics. *Quarterly of Quran & Medicine, 1*(1), 1–4.

Muhammad, A., Qayyum, Z., Mirza, W., Tanveer, S., Martinez-Enriquez, A. M., & Syed, A. (2012). E-Hafiz: Intelligent System to Help Muslims in Recitation and Memorization of Qúran. *Life Science Journal, 9*(1), 534–541. http://www.lifesciencesite.com

Mujica-Sequera, R. (2015, August). *Los obstáculos en el aprendizaje.* https://blog.docentes20.com/2015/08/los-obstaculos-en-el-aprendizaje-2/ (Accessed on November, 2023).

Neisser, U. (2014). *Cognitive psychology: Classic edition* (1st ed.). Psychology Press. https://doi.org/10.4324/9781315736174

Nowell, L. S., Norris, J. M., White, D. E., & Moules, N. J. (2017). Thematic analysis: Striving to meet the trustworthiness criteria. *International Journal of Qualitative Methods, 16*(1), 1–13. https://doi.org/10.1177/1609406917733847

Omar, T. (2017). Culture and Second Language Acquisition: Arabic Language as a Model. *European Scientific Journal, 13*(3), 159–166. https://doi.org/10.19044/esj.2016.v13n2p159

Olatoye, R. M. (2013). *Towards understanding the Islamic concept of the heart and its relationship with man's intention/actions.* In *Proceedings of the 1st Annual International Interdisciplinary Conference (AIIC 2013)* (pp. 183–189).

Osborne, L. (2020). The Mediated Qur'an: Religious Education and Recitation via Online Distance Learning in the Sultanate of Oman. *Yale Journal of Music & Religion, 6*(2 Sound and Secularity), Article 5. pp. 74–88. https://doi.org/10.17132/2377-231x.1170

Pastor, C. (2015). Guests of Islam: Conversion and the institutionalization of Islam in Mexico. In M. del M. Logroño, P. Pinto, & J. Tofik (Eds.), *Crescent Over Another Horizon. Islam in Latin America, The Caribbean and Latino USA* (First, p. 337). University of Texas Press.

Patton, M. Q. (2002). *Qualitative research and evaluation methods* (3rd ed.). Sage Publications, Inc.

Pedraza, S. A. (2015). *Buscando el Verdadero Mensaje del Islam en las Traducciones al Español del Sagrado Corán.* Retrieved from https://d1.islamhouse.com/data/es/ih_books/single/es_Buscando_el_verdadero_mensaje_de_Islam.pdf (Accessed on July 4, 2022)

Perry, B., & Winfrey, O. (2021). *What Happened to You? Conversations on Trauma, Resilience, and Healing* (First ed.). Flatiron Books.

PEW Research Center. (2012). *The global religious landscape: A report on the size and distribution of the world's major religious groups as of 2010.* Retrieved from https://assets.pewresearch.org/wp-content/uploads/sites/11/2012/12/globalReligion-tables.pdf (Accessed on November 5, 2024)

Ryan, R. M., & Deci, E. L. (2000). Intrinsic and Extrinsic Motivations: Classic Definitions and New Directions. *Contemporary Educational Psychology, 25*(1), 54–67.

Schön, D. (1998). *El Profesional Reflexivo. Cómo Piensan los Profesionales Cuando Actúan.* Paidós.

Şeker, M. Y. (2012). *A Map of the Divine Subtle Faculty: The Concept of Qalb (Heart) in Classical and Contemporary Islamic Scholarship* (Doctoral Thesis) [Australian Catholic University]. https://doi.org/10.4226/66/5a962c67c6893

Serrano, C. (November, 2013). *Fonética*. Asir Laymun. Retrieved from http://surl.li/cnfti (Accesssed on June 30, 2022).

Shekha, M. S., Hassan, A. O., & Othman, S. A. (2013). Effects of Quran Listening and Music on Electroencephalogram Brain Waves. *The Egyptian Society of Experimental Biology*, *9*(1), 1–7. http://www.egyseb.org

Smart, J. J. C. (2022). The Mind/Brain Identity Theory. In *Stanford Encyclopedia of Philosophy* (Winter 202). Edward N. Zalta & Uri Nodelman (eds.). Retrieved from https://plato.stanford.edu/entries/mind-identity/ (Accessed on July 8, 2023).

Smartech Solutions. (2022). *Tebyan Quran*. Prince Faisal bin Abdulrahman Al-Saud. Retrieved from https://tebyanquran.com (Accessed on November, 2023).

Soto Kiewit, L. D., Segura Jiménez, A., Navarro Rojas, Ó., Cedeño Rojas, S., & Medina Díaz, R. (2023). Educación formal, no formal e informal y la innovación: Innovar para educar y educar para innovar. *Innovaciones Educativas*, *25*(38), 77–96. https://doi.org/10.22458/ie.v25i38.4535

Souroujon, G. (2011). Reflexiones en Torno a la Relación entre Memoria, Identidad e Imaginación. *Andamios*, *8*(17), 233–257.

Supriyadi, T., & Julia, J. (2019). The Problem of Students in Reading the Quran: A Reflective-Critical Treatment Through Action Research. *International Journal of Instruction*, *12*(1), 311–326. https://doi.org/10.29333/iji.2019.12121a

Torres, B. (2013). La voz y nuestro cuerpo: un análisis funcional. *Revista de Investigaciones En Técnica Vocal*, *1*(0), 40–58. Retrieved from https://revistas.unlp.edu.ar/RITeV/article/

download/2059/4346/+&cd=28&hl=es&ct=clnk&gl=pe (Accessed on July, 2022).

Umm Máyid. (2015). *Reglas del Tajwid.* Retrieved from https://islamenespanol.files.wordpress.com/2015/02/reglas-del-tajwid.pdf
(Accessed on July 10, 2022).

Umm Najm. (2013). *Tajwid en Español Lecciones en cómo pronunciar el Corán.* Retrieved from https://taywid.wordpress.com/tag/tajweed-in-spanish/
(Accessed on July 10, 2022).

Vroon-Najem, V. (2014). *Sisters in Islam: Women's Conversion and the Politics of Belonging - A Dutch Case Study* (Doctoral Thesis) University of Amsterdam. Retrieved from http://dare.uva.nl/document/519090 (Accesses on January 2021).

Wadlinger, H., & Isaacowitz, D. (2011). Fixing our Focus: Training attention to regulate emotion. *Personality and Social Psychology Review, 15*(1), 75–102. https://doi.org/10.1177/1088868310365565.

Wahid, F. N., Norman, H., Nordin, N., Baharudin, H., Aziz, R., & Ibrahim, R. (2019). Designing an Online Quranic Recitation (Qirā'āt) Framework Using Massive Open Online Courses. *Creative Education, 10,* 3153–3162. https://doi.org/10.4236/ce.2019.1012239.

www.ingramcontent.com/pod-product-compliance
Lightning Source LLC
LaVergne TN
LVHW090046160826
845672LV00015B/1583